ELECTRIFY
YOUR STRINGS

The Mark Wood Improvisational Violin Method

By Mark Wood

To access audio visit:
www.halleonard.com/mylibrary
Enter Code
"3138-8855-1400-6330"

Cover art by Levin Pfeufer

Photos by Mark Weiss

Recording Credits:
Mark Wood, Violins and Keyboards
Laura Kaye, Vocals
T.M. Stevens, Bass
Jeff Plate, Drums
Eddie Rogers, Drums
Jon Bivona, Guitar
Paul Ranieri, Bass

ISBN: 978-1-57560-743-6

Visit Hal Leonard Online at
www.halleonard.com

CONTENTS

ABOUT THE AUTHOR

In an industry where originality is a highly prized commodity, recording artist, performer, producer, inventor, and Emmy-winning composer Mark Wood is truly an original. He began his career with a full scholarship to the prestigious Juilliard School in New York, and had the privilege of studying under maestro Leonard Bernstein at Tanglewood.

As an electric violinist, Mark Wood is a highly acclaimed international recording artist who has released six albums of his original music, showcasing his unique approach to the electric violin while playing on his own line of patented instruments.

He has toured and recorded with many of the industry's most prominent performers. In addition to touring with Celine Dion, he is featured on a duet with her on the song "To Love You More"; Mark was also the string arranger on two of her records. He is the featured violinist in Billy Joel's video for his song "All About Soul," appeared on *MTV Unplugged* with Lenny Kravitz, and has performed with Everclear in a live special for New York radio station WPLJ-FM. Mark is also the lead violinist and one of the original members of the multi-platinum–selling symphonic rock group Trans-Siberian Orchestra. Mark tours with an amazing group of musicians; his band, The Mark Wood Experience, features members of the Trans-Siberian Orchestra and vocalist Laura Kaye, who collaborates with Mark and appears on several of his albums.

In his capacity as composer, Mark started Mark Wood Music Productions, a company that focuses mainly on creating dramatic and inspirational pieces for television and film markets—particularly sports productions, network specials, and commercial spots. He received his first Emmy for the music he composed for CBS-TV's coverage of the 2002 Tour de France, and has received three additional Emmy nominations for his music for the 1992 Winter Olympics on CBS-TV, the documentary *Tim McCarver's World of Adventure* for ABC-TV, and for the 2003 Tour de France. His client list includes many of the major television networks as well as several world-famous recording artists. One of Mark's commissions was from The Juilliard School, which enlisted him to compose "Nest of Vipers" for their electric string quartet; the piece had its world premiere in April 2003 at Lincoln Center.

As an inventor, Mark established Wood Violins, a company whose mission is to make his instruments available to the general public. Wood Violins has become highly successful in custom-manufacturing and selling the patented Viper electric violin. This violin features a self-supporting mechanism that enables the instrumentalist to play without using a chin rest or shoulder pad. Wood Violins also manufactures the Sabre and the Stingray, both of which feature the traditional chin rest and shoulder pad, plus the self-supporting Cobra cello and Boa bass.

As educators across the country are quickly catching on to the importance of incorporating improvisation into their curricula, Mark's "Electrify Your Strings" education programs have become highly successful. EYS has been brought to hundreds of schools from coast to coast, including the Berklee School of Music, the Juilliard School, Oneonta University, the Rock and Roll Hall of Fame, and many others. He is also an instructor of a special course at the annual Mark O'Connor Fiddle Camps held in Nashville and San Diego, and hosts his own Mark Wood Music Camp during the summer. Additionally, Mark is a New York Foundation for the Arts grant recipient.

Mark's solo releases include *These Are a Few of My Favorite Things* (a compilation of the best of his hard-rock violin catalogue, with highlights such as his versions of "Eleanor Rigby" and "Purple Haze"), *Portrait of an Artist* (modern classical compositions for double-string quartet, percussion, and voice inspired by the works of his father, abstract painter Paul Wood), *Sanctuary* (a collaboration with singer/songwriter Laura Kaye that includes several members of Celine Dion's band), *Voodoo Violince, Against the Grain, Music from the Tour de France,* as well as *Guts, Grace & Glory* and *Guts, Grace & Glory II.* In 2005, he produced and performed on *Shake Off the Gravity* for Laura Kaye.

In 2007, Mark performed in the world premiere of "Viper Versus Orchestra" in New York's Carnegie Hall. He is currently starring in a national television ad campaign for Pepsi. The music track is a Kanye West–produced hip-hop version of "The Devil Went Down to Georgia" featuring the rapper Nas.

You can find more much information about Mark on the web.

Mark Wood:
www.markwoodmusic.com
www.facebook.com/markwoodmusic

Wood Violins:
www.woodviolins.com
www.facebook.com/woodviolins

Electrify Your Strings:
www.electrifyyourstrings.com (Visit this site to find even more cool exercises, solos, and information!)
www.facebook.com/electrifyyourstrings

He can be reached via email at info@markwoodmusic.com, and via phone at (516) 767-6677.

Mark Live with the Trans-Siberian Orchestra

ACKNOWLEDGMENTS

It always takes a tremendous amount of energy and people power to move mountains. The first person I would like to thank is John Stix. This is the second time he has given me the gift of a platform in order to showcase my work. The first opportunity came in the form of producing my debut record *Voodoo Violince*, which changed the way we hear the violin. The second is now, with the publication of this method book that will change the way people think in terms of learning to play the violin. Thanks, John!

Thanks to Susan Poliniak who worked harder than 50 people on this book. Thanks for your faith in me and your dedication to helping me express my concepts.

Thanks to Mark O'Connor, Matt Glaser, Philip Pan, Jay Labore, Val Vigoda, Bridgid Bibbens, ASTA, Mike Gagliardo, all our Viper Vixens, Alyson Montez, Joe Domjan and everyone at Wood Violins, the mighty Trans-Siberian Orchestra, and all the great players and people who are part of our Wood Violins message board and online community.

Thanks to all the school string teachers I've worked with over the years in my Electrify Your Strings music education program. Together we will inspire students all over the world to empower themselves with music!

Special thanks to my wonderful parents, my three brothers, and, of course last but not least, my partner/wife/ awesome singer Laura Kaye, and my rockin' drummer/violinist/lighting designer son Elijah.

INTRODUCTION

Art is a constantly evolving mode of expression, an organic force that continuously challenges and inspires us. Music, in particular, has the power to transform and elevate those who participate in its creation, as well as those who enjoy the fruits of its creators. From the Renaissance to the rock 'n' roll era, we have enjoyed supporting and celebrating our artists and innovators as they evolve and change the creative landscape.

This book, geared toward both string educators and students alike, provides a fresh approach to the violin, an instrument that has been around for hundreds of years, and offers some insight into what I feel is the next step in its evolution. This instrument has made immense contributions to Western music during the last several hundred years—from the beautiful Bach violin and cello suites to the Philip Glass violin concerto, and from the great Baroque string players to the rock-star status of 19th-century violin virtuoso Nicolo Paganini.

Today, in many non-classical and alternative circles, string players are challenged to maintain the kind of status they had during Paganini's day. In fact, we have nowhere near the kind of influence on pop culture as we did before the industrial age. I am by no means saying that classical string playing in modern times is not "cool," but am merely trumpeting the existence of an alternative way of approaching the violin in the hopes that we as instrumentalists can reclaim our superhero status. Although we violinists know what a gift it is to be able to express ourselves through such an amazing instrument, the rock and pop worlds are constantly challenging us to "fit in," to come up with a new approach. It is time for us to become involved with the new string world order. The revolution has begun—it is time to plug in, improvise, and make new contributions to non-classical contemporary music!

Violinists should never compromise or discard the study and artistry of the classical idiom—its techniques are truly the strongest foundation we have as string players. However, are we losing the "point" of learning and teaching string music? When I travel to schools and universities around the country, giving lectures and workshops on my methods, I am astounded when I witness string virtuosos who cannot play a single note when you remove the sheet music in front of them! These musicians are great athletes on their instruments. Certainly, the joy of being able to play a Dvořàk string quartet or sight-read a Mozart sonata is the gift of a well-trained talent, but in this day and age we need to have broader educational methods at our disposal.

Traditionally trained string players are taught to play what they see, to express themselves through what is written on the page. While ear training is a traditional component of musical pedagogy, the development of improvisational skills has been largely ignored. By contrast, actors are trained to go "beyond the page"—when you remove their scripts, they can easily shift to an improvisational landscape. In everyday conversations, we are constantly improvising our thoughts, expressing ourselves in a most immediate way. We need to be equally improvisational as string players.

— Looking Back

Europeans who immigrated to the United States many years ago brought classical music with them. They set up symphony halls and conservatories that promoted and taught the styles from their respective cultures that, in turn, greatly influenced our collective musical experience. Yet a "new" music began to evolve right here in this country. Seeds from all over were planted which ultimately grew into styles such as jazz, pop, rock, folk, country, hip-hop, and so forth.

The massive musical and spiritual contributions from the African-American community still permeate much of our popular music and have inspired artists such as the Beatles, the Rolling Stones, and Led Zeppelin, among many others. I truly believe America's Mozarts and Beethovens are people such as Scott Joplin, Woody

Guthrie, Louis Armstrong, Duke Ellington, John Coltrane, Miles Davis, Frank Zappa, and Jimi Hendrix. There have been historical-geographic hotbeds of creativity. Musically, one can look at Vienna in the 1700s, and Paris in the early 1900s. The US had its own such creative burst from 1930 to 1979, with the advancements in jazz, Motown, rock, etc., and all of the artists who took part. This is America's great contribution to world musical history. Many years from now, this time period in American history will be looked upon as a huge explosion of art on the level of those that took place in Vienna and Paris in earlier times.

— Looking Forward

What is it about the invention of electricity that changed the musical world forever? Guitarists and keyboardists know the answer and have been exploring electrical avenues for over 50 years. String players are only now beginning to make the leap in a big way from acoustic to electric. In my opinion, the "big bang" in the guitar world happened when Jimi Hendrix played "The Star-Spangled Banner" at Woodstock in 1969. He used his instrument to create blaring feedback and explosions just like the rockets' red glare. My personal "big bang" in the violin world happened in two stages. The first was when I heard Don "Sugarcane" Harris play on a Frank Zappa record (*Weasels Ripped My Flesh*), and the second was when I started listening to the Mahavishnu Orchestra. That band featured Jerry Goodman on violin; he was the first rock violinist I heard that had truly "great" classical technique combined with the ability to make his violin totally rock out with wah-wah pedals and amplification. Inspired beyond words, I began to forge my own path in the electric violin world.

— My Story

I come from a family of musicians and artists. When I was growing up, I was surrounded by my three brothers who also played string instruments (we formed a string quartet and performed at many concerts), a mother who was a professional pianist, and a father who was an abstract artist, who himself came from a family of

woodworkers. Certainly, this was an incredible environment in which to grow up. Classical music was played often in our home and this is where I developed a great love and respect for it. But when I bumped into the Beatles, my musical life changed in an instant! Of course, my passion for classical music continues to this day, but back then I was blown away by musicians such as Emerson, Lake & Palmer, Gentle Giant, King Crimson, Frank Zappa, Yes, and other '70s progressive rock bands who created extremely exciting and fresh music that not only had a rock 'n' roll sensibility but also pushed the boundaries of a new "electric" classical music.

While my musical palette was expanding, I continued with a fairly strict classical background that included studying at Tanglewood with the Boston Symphony Orchestra and Leonard Bernstein, working with assorted private teachers, and attending the Juilliard School at age 16 on a full scholarship. At Juilliard, I had musical experiences that ran the gamut from phenomenal to dreadful. I had a very conservative viola teacher who, without realizing it, became the main catalyst in my decision to pursue my vision: becoming an electric violinist.

When I finally left Juilliard, I was a man on a mission. I desperately wanted to learn how to improvise and play the music I loved, which was rock and jazz. At the time, I could play the most complex classical music, but I couldn't improvise a note. There were no jazz or rock violin method books available so I taught myself by ear and closely observed and absorbed the techniques of the musicians I truly admired: Jimi Hendrix, Eddie Van Halen, John McLaughlin, Jean-Luc Ponty,

Robert Fripp, Jimmy Page, Steve Vai, Jerry Goodman, and many others. Through trial and error, I developed the concepts and theories you will find in this book.

— The Next Step: Inventing a Great Electric Violin

As far as redesigning the violin itself, that started when I was about 12 years old. Since there were no really cool looking and playable electric violins to chose from, I had no choice but to build my own by hand (my family owned a woodworking shop, so it was definitely in my blood). After several experimental efforts, I finally mastered the construction of these new and exciting instruments. I also discovered a new way of supporting the violin—I made an instrument that actually "floats!" I decided to get rid of the chin rest and shoulder pad and patented a support mechanism that enabled me to strap the instrument comfortably onto my body. This enables me to race around the stage and perform the way I envisioned.

— Become a Violin Hero!

Unlike the guitar world, which is constantly growing and embracing new techniques, the methods I was trained to follow in my conservative string education are pretty close to those still being used with students today. The typical path for a string player is to start on the instrument at age eight or nine, play in a school orchestra, get a private teacher, and perhaps go on to a conservatory for further study. But then what? The president of one of the more prestigious music schools in the USA recently cautioned string students *against* pursuing a career in music because of the lack of financial returns!

But I disagree—the time is ripe for optimism!

Music can be a great field to enter, and it's wide open for alternatively-trained string players. Every style of music—from country to jazz, blues to rock, Celtic to folk, even techno and beyond—can be a source of income and provide an exciting and viable career. Even if you're not pursuing a career in string playing, the methods outlined in this book can give you more emotional, expressive, and enjoyable playing experiences with your instrument.

With a growing number of string players exploring alternative styles, let's create that "big bang" in the string world! Guitar heroes are everywhere. We need more *modern violin* heroes!

— Educate Yourself

At long last, pedagogues are seeing that "alternative" styles can be important elements in the teaching of string technique—and students are eager to learn these new styles. Of course, while the strong technical foundation that classical training provides is essential for a lifetime of confident playing, the classical art form, as it is practiced today, can be limiting in that its focus is on interpretation and respecting the wishes of the composer. When musicians improvise, their personalities shine through. Through improvisation, we are able to channel the immediacy of our lives into the creation of our own music.

This is where my method comes in. Through it, we can model ourselves on musicians such as John Lennon, Miles Davis, Keith Richards, John Coltrane, Eric Clapton, Jimi Hendrix, Jeff Beck, Frank Zappa, and the countless others who have greatly influenced our modern musical styles. By the way, many of these musicians never studied music in conservatories—they each learned their craft mainly via their own ears and their passionate commitment to expressing their own personal artistry. If fact, whereas classical studies are based heavily on the student/teacher relationship, this new and exciting world of the alternate approach encourages the player to self-teach and develop a more personalized approach to their art.

— The Art of Creativity

The concept of child-like play is essential to improvising. Watching my young son at play is fascinating—I can actually witness him utilizing concepts such as form, order, and instant decision-making as they integrate with his imagination. These are all parts of improvisation no less than conversational skills. When we hold conversations with each other, we are accessing our thoughts and feelings and instantly converting them via technique (here, verbal) to communication. We as musicians must establish these sorts of connections in our own performance experiences. Spontaneity is the important element here.

— Speak with Your Own Voice

One musician who embodies a lot of the qualities I admire is violinist and composer Mark O'Connor. To me, he represents the ideal musician, balancing his gift for improvising while maintaining a concert violin career that includes writing and performing music that is both original and thought-provoking. He had rather unorthodox violin training with supreme success as a world-class fiddler and jazz violinist, eventually progressing into a successful "classical" career. In his case, his abilities to improvise are part of the core of his skills as a composer. Mark has honestly channeled his American influences into a beautiful hybrid of fiddle, jazz, and Celtic music, and melded that with the European tradition of the great violinists of the late 19th century.

— In Conclusion

I'm not interested in breeding string athletes—I'm only interested in nuturing musicians and creative thinkers. I'm also interested in strengthening our abilities as educators and students to form deeper connections with music and more meaningful relationships with our audiences. When I hear a song like "Imagine" by John Lennon I feel the "personal touch" in that music and its emotional impact is evident; it immediately speaks to a very deep part of my spirit. This underscores the power inherent in individual expression as opposed to moving into the common home for string players in the classical world, which is being stuck in the back of the second violin section of a 100-piece orchestra playing Bruckner's Symphony No. 5 for the 50th time!

The ability of people to "touch" each other emotionally is one of the most important and wonderful aspects of our existence. Whether playing alone in a room, or in front of 50,000 people, musicians have a responsibility to connect with each other and their audience and touch them with their music. The style of music is not as important as the connection, but if you want to access the quickest and most concise route, improvisation is a great start.

— About This Book

This book will introduce both educators and students to a new violin pedagogy that can help to develop a certain kind of musicianship. This method contains the tools I developed for myself to help me to gain the skills needed for my musical vision. The instruction here is a great starting point, but it is not the be-all and end-all. Nothing is!

Play creatively! Live creatively!

Note: The following tuning pitches are included. Each note is played three times.

Chapter 1

The Fretted Violin: The Moveable-Frame Fingerboard Grid

— A Template for Improvising

When you look at a violin, viola, or cello fingerboard, you see a blank canvas. Playing a fretless instrument is always a challenging and stimulating experience. Yet, with new technologies available and new musical demands placed upon us, we must address every aspect of string playing and push the boundaries.

In other words, we shouldn't be afraid of the concept of *frets*.

Whether you are attracted to the physical feeling of a fret under your fingers or just thinking and visualizing the fret grid on your fretless fingerboard—or even whether you like or dislike actual steel frets—this chapter is an important step to unlocking the mysteries of your fingerboard. And, yes, you can play any style of music with frets, including classical music. In fact, playing the music of Bach with frets can allow you to truly appreciate his skills as a composer for the keyboard.

String players, with their fretless instruments, spend a large part of their practice time on improving their sense of intonation. Although developing a great sense of pitch for any musician is essential, thinking in terms of frets can allow an instrumentalist to spend more time *actually playing music*.

On a guitar or a keyboard instrument, the fingerboard and keys, respectively, are arranged according to a very specific layout that corresponds to certain notes. This same concept can be applied to bowed string instruments with the use of frets.

It's not difficult to incorporate the idea of frets into your musical world. The first step is simply to visualize frets on your fingerboard. This is an important first step toward incorporating the new concepts of improvisation and non-classical music styles into your practice.

If you own a traditional, acoustic string instrument, let's set up a start point. You do not need to put markings at every half step point on your fingerboard. Just apply a thin piece of colored tape to these key areas:

1. First position, first finger
2. Third position, first finger
3. Fourth position, first finger
4. 12th position, first finger (octave harmonic)

In other words, if you're looking just at the G string, the tape would be at the A (first position), C (third position), D (fourth position), and G octave harmonic (12th position). Remember that at the 12th "fret" the fingerboard is split in exactly half; this is where the main harmonic (octave) lies.

If you'd feel more comfortable with actual frets, my company Wood Violins manufactures fretted violins and cellos. We also make something called "invisible frets," which are fret markings up and down the fingerboard without the "bump" of regular frets.

If you do own one of our fretted instruments, you'll notice that the fingerboard includes dots.

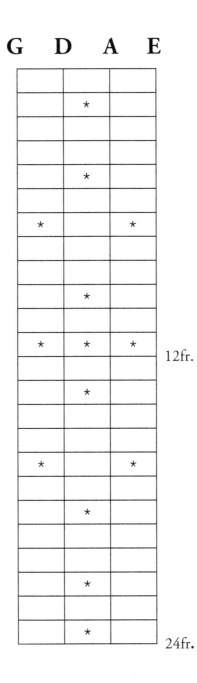

The configuration of these dots is very specific; they are positioned between fretwires. as they are on guitar necks. Note that when you play a bowed instrument with frets, you should place your left-hand finger(s) *on top of* a fret, not *behind* it as on a guitar.

— The Octave Hand Position

Because the violin, the viola, and the cello are tuned in 5ths, the octave hand position is a specific form that works up and down (as well as across) the fingerboard. This position on the violin and the viola involves the 1st finger and the 4th finger on two neighboring strings. In other words, the notes under your 1st and 4th fingers on adjacent strings (lower and higher, respectively) form an octave, as shown below.

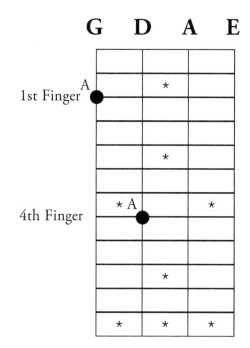

Now, think of this position moving horizontally across and vertically up and down the fingerboard, responding to different key changes and scale forms. Utilize the same finger pattern as often as possible as you move this position around. When you need to transpose or change keys, use your 1st finger as the *root* (the note on which the key is based—G in G major, for example) of the key or riff.

— Your First Experience in Improvising!

Let's jam over one chord—Am. Place your hand in 1st position, forming the octave hand position on the G and D strings. Using no open strings, play the A minor pentatonic scale: A–C–D–E–G. Notice that the fingering is 1–3–4–1–3–4 (adding that octave A in for good measure), and that the A notes are circled below.

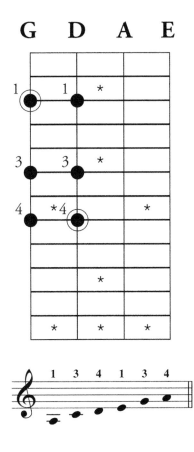

Since you have only five notes to worry about, start playing variations and patterns on just these specific notes—and notice that all of the notes "work" over Am!

  Here's an example of what I would play.

You'll notice, by the way, that the audio is *split-channel*. My solo is on the left side of the stereo field (in your left speaker) and the accompaniment track is on the right side. This way, you can adjust your stereo so you can hear just what I'm doing, or just the accompaniment so you can create your own masterpiece!

In the chapters to come, you will study the subject of improvisation in depth (and in the next chapter, you'll see much more material on pentatonic scales!). Once you've mastered the fret grid concept, you will be able to "evolve" from this starting point of the octave hand position and develop your own fingerings. Try not to use any open strings on the improvisation exercises so you can maintain a specific finger pattern for your first ventures into the world of frets.

— Arpeggios

To further reinforce the octave hand position concept, the next step is to learn how to "spell" different chord configurations. The following exercise includes a selection of chords with roots based on A, B, and C. Begin with the A exercises in first position. The first finger should be on the root with your other fingers forming the octave hand position Once you have mastered the pattern in A, move your hand up to 2nd position for B. Then, move the frame up a half step for C. When you feel confident with the written examples, go "beyond the page" and play the chords based on C♯, D, D♯, and so on. This is an important exercise, as the arpeggios set up the "skeletons" of different scale options. From the major scale configurations to the minor and 7th chord scale configurations, you can easily see the outlines of lots of different scales within the octave hand position.

TRACK 03

Here are grids for some chords based on A.

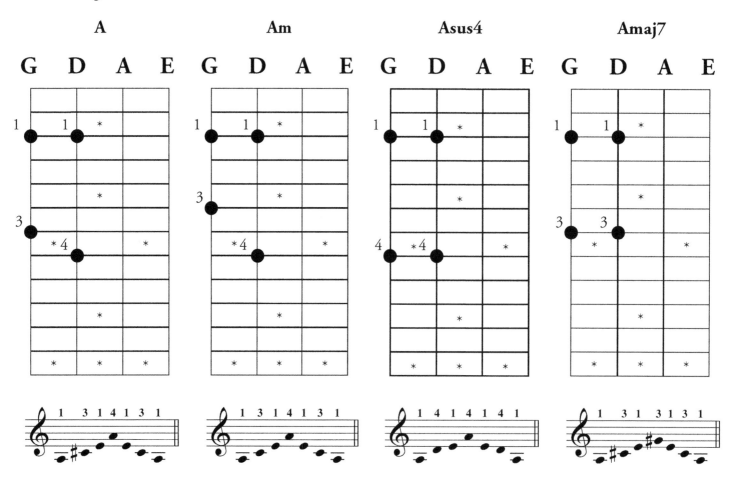

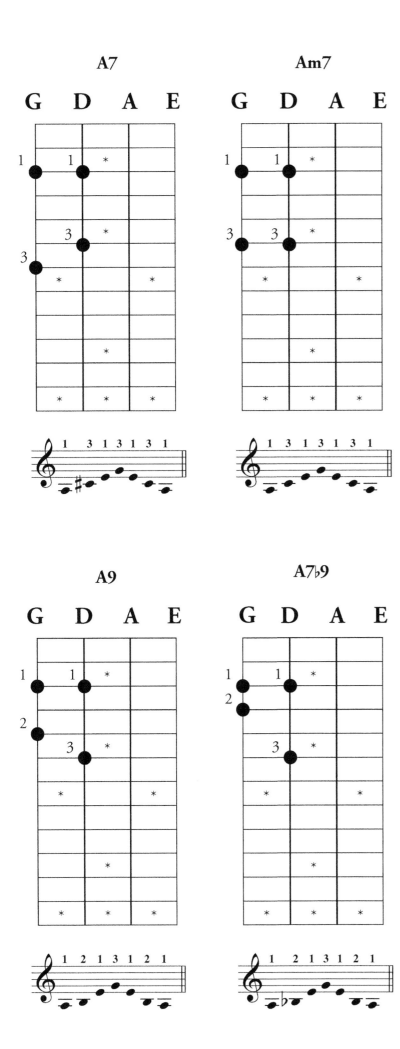

I've been playing a fretted electric violin for over 20 years—in fact, I was probably one of the first on the instrument—and have found through it a new and exciting way to handle my musical vision and voice. While my acoustic violin will always give me the pleasure of playing fretless, it is important to me to investigate and explore as many new and radical concepts as I can on my "new" violin. One of the great surprise benefits that I discovered from putting frets on a violin is that these frets do not hinder the beautiful nuances of an acoustic violin (i.e., slides, bends, vibrato). When you strum the fretted violin like a mandolin, the frets act just like they do on a guitar; if your finger is placed behind the fret the pitch remains the same. But once the bow hits the string, the frets sort of "disengage" the pitch-locking concept of a guitar fret and what happens is that the frets act more like a visual grid and mapping system, yet still provide excellent pitch clarification everywhere on the fingerboard.

The pitch of a note actually "resides" on the top of its fret; in other words, you finger a note in this way. This allows you to play more in tune and gives you the ability to explore chordal work. And, yes, you can still play microtones and utilize traditional violin techniques with frets!

The frets also set up a visual architecture that I use when I compose music. It's similar to the visual landscape of the piano when used as a compositional tool. Another advantage to these frets as visual markers is that during a live performance when you are struggling to hear yourself above the volume of a band, you can glance at your fingerboard for visual guidance.

What I've found to be so eye-opening about the concept of frets is how they make me think about my instrument in fresh, new ways. Frets have opened my mind to new ways of approaching and performing on my violin. In turn, my violin has become more than just a stringed instrument—it is now a powerful composition tool. And this is where the future lies for us as consummate improvisers.

You can apply all of the information in this chapter to a fretless violin. There are certainly physical differences between fretted and fretless instruments. I, personally, play differently on a fretless violin. The important thing is to remember that our mission is to have more options for our creative endeavors!

Some Thoughts from Other Players

Philip Pan, Concertmaster of the Jacksonville Symphony Orchestra

"You can totally ignore the frets if and when you want to and play any style, any pitches you want to including high sharps, low flats, Bartók microtones—anything! So they don't act like training wheels unless you look at them and use them that way. Think you'll ever play with a loud band where you'll need to really crank up your volume just to be heard? Think you'll ever want to join in music already playing and nail the first note? Well, then, you'll love having frets. I'm almost willing to bet that, while you can drop your fingers real darn close to the right pitch just by muscle memory, you have been doing what virtually all acoustic players do to get your first note dead in-tune: You listen to the quiet sound made as you drop your finger on the string, right before you play it. When you do that with your volume set really high, everyone in the room hears it, too! But if you aim for a fret, you don't have to test the note before you play it, assuming the Viper is in tune. You just put your finger right on it with confidence.

"Another thing you can run into if you have absolute pitch and good muscle memory: What if you are doing a transposed or scordatura tuning? That's a situation that drives those of us with absolute pitch bananas because your fingers betray your intentions when you're tuned, say, a half step down and fingering the piece in A but the song is in A♭. Once again, frets will really help, especially with nailing the first note.

"Those are my main uses for frets, plus I'm convinced that they increase clarity and articulation on the lower strings. 99.9% of the time, I find my notes purely by ear and feel, but that 0.1% of the time when you can't do that, the frets are so vital. And when you're jumping up to high positions on the Viper, its physical references are completely different from an acoustic fiddle's. Without 'shoulders,' you can easily flip your hand up to 7th position or beyond and back without having to 'climb around' the body of the instrument hardly at all. But if you are used to finding a high position by feel from years of acoustic training, that will all go out the window on a Viper. Frets can be very useful here too."

Val Vigoda, Electric Violinist from the Band GrooveLily

"As a classical violinist who has played for many years without frets, I can say unquestionably that I LOVE having frets. The great thing about the frets is that they don't prevent you from doing any of the things you could do without them (slides, glissandos, etc.). It doesn't really even feel very different. To me, the frets are more of a visual aid since they're so short and sanded down, but they definitely help with intonation, especially on the lower strings (the ones I wasn't used to from my years of playing a four-string). I also love the fact that the frets can help you think more chordally, like a guitar player, rather than just linearly and melodically like other violinists.

"I got my first six-string, fretted Viper in 1996, and my second one in 1999. What I do in my band GrooveLily involves quite a bit of singing and playing simultaneously, and the frets help me with that enormously. Also, if you're ever in a band situation where you can't hear yourself that well on stage, having frets and at least SEEING that you're close to the right note can help your confidence!

Jay Labore, String Teacher

"Frets on a violin?! Why not?

First—and I fear that I will have some classical musicians mad at me on this—but fretted violins and cellos have been done before. I had a reference at my old mentor's desk that had pictures of some very old instruments with frets.

"I think the reason why frets weren't used widely until Mark came on the scene is simply because string players are all stuck in the old ways. It's the same reason why we won't put tuning machines in place of pegs. It's the same reason why the violin doesn't have a 5th string on it to compensate for the lack of the hard-to-find viola player. Some have said that making changes to the violin will change its sounds, or just kill the tradition. Well, look at it like this: Try opening a general store with a register from 1880 and no credit card machine!

"We need to adapt our craft to society. Biplanes and frigates are gone. Jets and nuclear-powered aircraft carriers are in.

"The frets and design associated with Mark's Vipers allow for an old instrument like the violin to meld into new music. They facilitate chord work, and that is a big thing because we must be able to take the rhythm chair and not be just melody-only instruments.

"Try playing a 12-bar blues chord progression in A on three or more strings on violins both with frets and without. No matter how good you are, it's nice to have those frets there so you can relax on the concentration and just play.

"After using instruments with frets, I have discovered that my large shift jumps have DRASTICALLY increased in accuracy! Also, I am significantly lighter with my touch with my regular instruments, which is a good thing. Any good violin player will tell you that you don't want to press too hard on the strings. A common playing issue is what I call 'squeezing the feathers out of the neck.' Tone quality, playing speed, and stamina all come from how much finesse you put into your fingering. I always thought I had a pretty light touch on my strings, and then I played the fretted Viper. I have discovered that I barely have to touch the strings on those frets in order to get my slides, vibrato, etc. So, after playing for so much time, I went to my regular, 'non-fretted' instruments, and without even thinking, I was pressing down on the strings so much lighter than before and was getting an even nicer tone. Just goes to show, you think you are doing things right for so many years . . ."

"The distance between the frets is comparable to the spacing on a traditional unfretted violin. The 'feel' might be different at first, but it's something that your fingers and your ear adapt to. The frets are flat—kind of like thick metallic finger-tapes— and not high and rounded like on a guitar. You can see the frets as you look down the length of the instrument, and although they don't stick up very high off the fingerboard, you can just feel them under the strings.

"For a beginner, frets offer a positive marker for pitch-correctness. This is not cheating, so get that out of your head. Pitch accuracy will help increase success and, hence, confidence for the beginning player."

CHAPTER 2

THE MINOR PENTATONIC SCALE

Pentatonic scales are a great place to start with improvising.

The minor pentatonic scale is a five-note scale (hence "penta") that is used often in rock and blues music. It is the foundation of the blues scale, among others. This pentatonic scale is great as-is, but it also "sets up" the basic hand position and note pattern system on which other scales are based.

Here it is, in reference to the notes of a major scale: 1–♭3–4–5–♭7. Beginning on A, it's A–C–D–E–G. Try playing the scale as written below, paying attention to the fingerings. This scale may look a little familiar to you—it's the one that was used in the previous chapter for the improvisation exercise!

It is extremely important that you master the minor pentatonic scales in as many keys and octaves as possible. With this scale under your fingers, you will have in your possession an extremely valuable improvisational tool. The exercises below can help you to build your skills in this department.

— Scale Exercises for the Four-String Violin

No matter what, always pay attention to the fingerings, bowings, and articulations!

Once you feel confident playing any of these exercises along with me, try playing them along to a metronome or simple drum loop, or to the backing track for each exercise.

— Minor Pentatonic Scale Exercise #1: Quarter Notes over One Octave

TRACK 04

— Minor Pentatonic Scale Exercise #2: Eighth Notes over Two Octaves

TRACK 05

— Minor Pentatonic Scale Exercise #3: 16th Notes over Two Octaves

This exercise is set up like an actual riff for the purpose of showing you the possibilities of the minor pentatonic scale in a more "real-life" musical context.

— Minor Pentatonic Scale Exercise #4: Ascending and Descending Eighth Note Triplets

This is the first of three exercises involving minor pentatonic eighth note triplet patterns. All of these are excellent warm-ups, and these exercises can really help you straighten out your upbow/downbow issues, if you have any. The odd note groupings force you to work on activating both strong downbow and upbow strokes.

— Minor Pentatonic Scale Exercise #5: More Ascending and Descending Eighth Note Triplets

— Minor Pentatonic Scale Exercise #6: Even More Ascending and Descending Eighth Note Triplets

— Minor Pentatonic Scale Exercise #7: Long Eighth Note Scale Riff

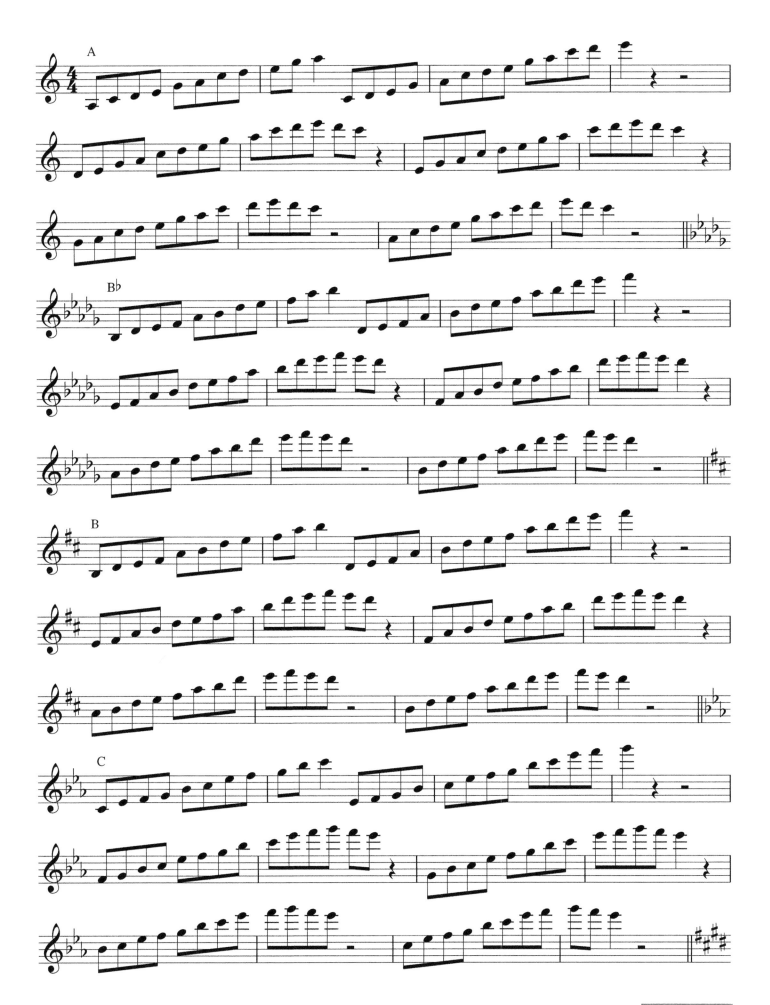

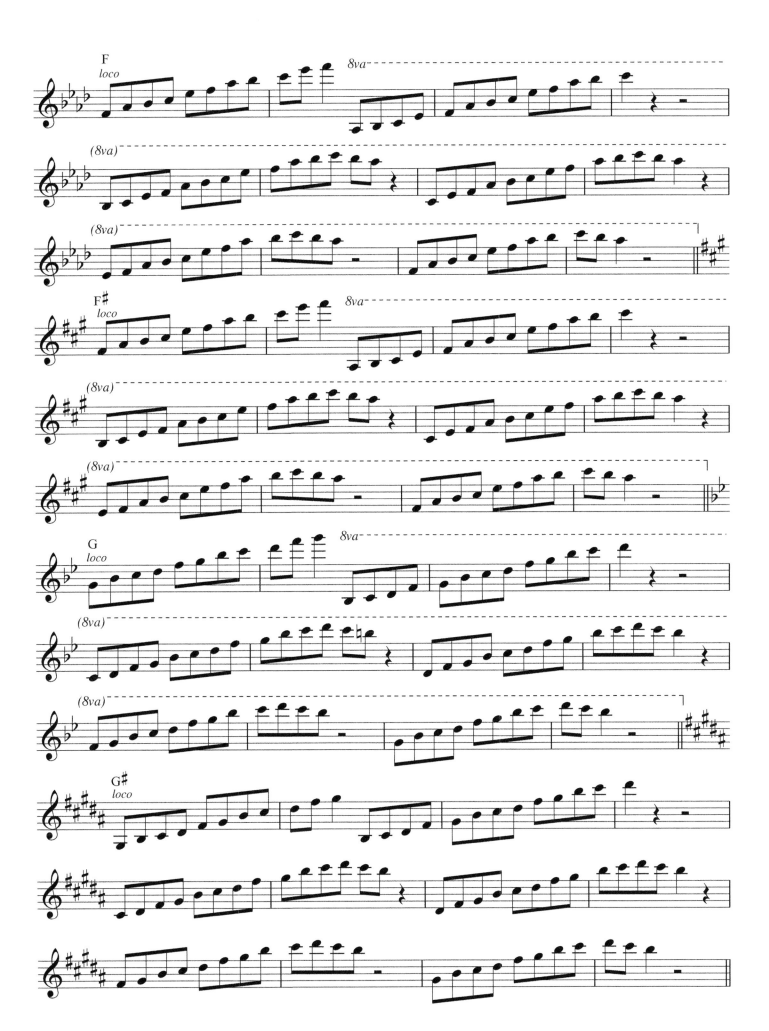

— Minor Pentatonic Scale Exercise #8: Eighth Notes over Two Octaves in Different Positions

This exercise approaches the A minor pentatonic scale via different positions. This is the next step in the "movable frame" concept (the first being the octave hand position). Here, the A minor pentatonic scale starts on each successive note of the scale in each line of the exercise. When you have this down, transpose it to other keys by moving your hand position on the neck.

— Minor Pentatonic Scale Exercise #9: Scale in A over One Octave in Three Different Positions

Here, you begin on the root each time, but in different octaves.

1st Position

8th Position

— Minor Pentatonic Scale Exercise #10: First-Position Scales over One Octave in G, D, and A

— Scale Exercises for Five-, Six-, and Seven-String Violins

These next three exercises are for those of you who play violins that have more than four strings. Note that we're starting on the lowest note possible in the A minor pentatonic scale, not the root.

— Minor Pentatonic Scale Exercise #11: Quarter Notes over Two Octaves for the Five-String Violin

— Minor Pentatonic Scale Exercise #12: Quarter Notes over Two Octaves for the Six-String Violin

1st Position

2nd Position

3rd Position

— Minor Pentatonic Scale Exercise #13: Quarter Notes over Two Octaves for the Seven-String Violin

1st Position

2nd Position

3rd Position

CHAPTER 3

THE BLUES SCALE AND THE 12-BAR BLUES

— The Blues Scale

You can think of the blues scale as a sort of "continuation" of the minor pentatonic scale. In order to create a blues scale, just add a ♭5 into a minor pentatonic scale so it looks like this: 1–♭3–4–♭5–65–♭7. Below, the blues scale in A is written out for you in the form of an exercise. Transpose the scale by moving your hand around the neck, using the same fingerings for each key as shown below.

TRACK 07

— The 12-Bar Blues

Playing improvisations with a blues scale over a 12-bar blues progression is the best way to *really* learn the scale—and it's not a bad way to learn the progression either! The 12-bar blues is the foundation for a lot of rock tunes. The basic progression in A major looks like this.

TRACK 08

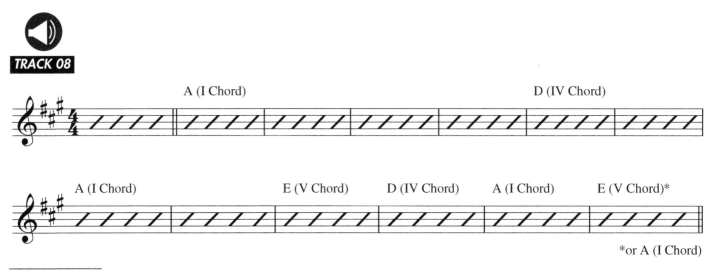

*or A (I Chord)

Often in the last measure, right before the progression repeats, you'll hear a V chord instead of a I chord. This ending of a blues progression is called a *turnaround* because, literally, it "turns the progression around" to its beginning. On the recording, the V chord (E) is used in the turnaround, which then resolves to the I in the beginning of the next *chorus* (one full trip through the 12 bars of a blues progression), or in a little coda at the very end.

— The Bow Blues Shuffle

Now, here's an example of what I would do over a blues in A, using the A blues scale. Measures 23–30 and 49–51 have some nice standard riffs that you can incorporate into your own playing.

Did you notice that "bouncy" rhythmic feel? It's different than the feel of the previous blues chorus. This new one is in what's called a *shuffle feel, swing feel,* or *triplet feel,* and it's very common in blues, jazz, and rock music. Pairs of eighth notes are treated as though they were the first and third members of an eighth note triplet. You'll see this sort of feel indicated by a note at the beginning of the music which says "swing feel," "shuffle feel," or "triplet feel," and/or a little bit of notation showing you that two eighth notes are to be played as the first and third parts of a eighth note triplet.

Try soloing yourself over the rhythm section—remember, the accompaniment is in the right channel of the track! At first, try playing what I played. When you feel confident with that, try improvising your own solo using notes from the A blues scale: A–C–D–E♭–E♮–G.

— Rock Your Bow!

Here's another blues in E. This time, I've added several notes that go *beyond* the standard blues scale. These are the major 2nd (F♯), the major 3rd (G♯), the major 6th (C♯), and minor 6th (C) of the E major scale. The minor 3rd sounds great leading into the major 3rd, the major and minor 6ths work really well around the 5th, and the major 2nd is a member of the V chord (B).

Rock on!

TRACK 10

Now, improvise a solo of your own over the rhythm section using the E blues scale. When you're confident with that, feel free to throw in any of those "extra" notes! Start playing around with the major 3rd first, then the 6ths, and then that major 2nd.

— String Thang

The following is an example of what I would do over a 12-bar blues in E major on a seven-string, fretted Viper. (I've added in octave down pedal markings so you can play this on a four-string violin.) This one has more of a rock feel and includes the use of distortion, echo, and wah-wah (there's more information on each of these effects later in the book). Use the E minor blues scale throughout. Notice that there are short "stops" in the rhythm section here. The usual chords still apply—the progression is no different—but the silence affords you an opportunity to be a little more creative with your improv ideas when you tackle it on your own.

— Straight Shooter Blues

This one is another blues in A, but this time with a different feel. Whereas the previous blues in A had a shuffle feel, this one is in straight eighths. Have a listen to what I do, and then try your own solo!

TRACK 12

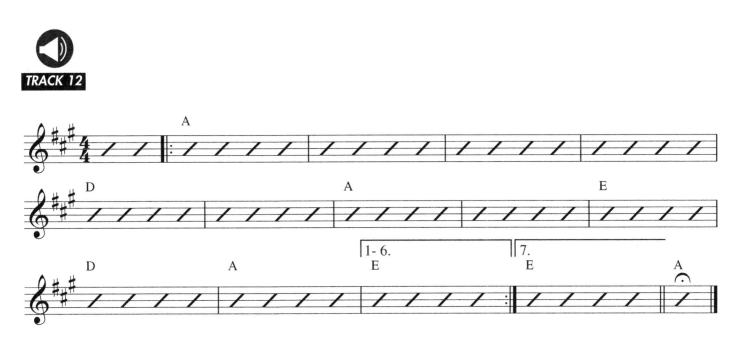

CHAPTER 4

PLAYING RHYTHM

Most beginners, when they first get into blues, rock, jazz and other non-classical styles, want to jump ahead and work on just soloing and playing lead, but you really need to learn how to play rhythm as well. Many people think of bowed strings as being monophonic or solo instruments only, but they make excellent rhythm instruments, too. It's beneficial for violinists to develop their skills in this department. Playing lead is all well and good, but you should be able to play solid backup and have the sound of the chords in your head. In contemporary music people are expecting and demanding more from our sting players, and the more skills you have under your fingers, the better.

— Feeling Rhythm

Music is alive. It has a heartbeat, which is the pulse of the rhythmic feel. As you approach these exercises, make sure that you tap your foot. *Feel* the rhythm in your body. Also, the use of a metronome is recommended so you can really lock into the beat properly.

— Rhythm Techniques and Chords

Chopping, scraping, bouncing the bow, left-hand pizzicato, rolling bass lines, sweep bowings, and more allow you to get a variety of feels for the creation of a solid rhythmic groove.

Since the violin, viola, and cello are tuned in 5ths, their tunings themselves are an excellent start point for new voicings and chord configurations. Most chords include a 5th, which automatically gives you a great left-hand form—you just place your fingers on the same fret on two strings simultaneously and you have a 5th!

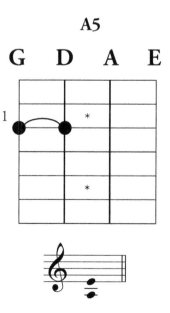

The 5th above is, as you can see, labeled "A5." This is the notation for a *power chord*. Simply (and obviously!) put, a power chord is a root plus its 5th, and you find it all over the place in rock and heavy metal music.

Chords include 5ths, 3rds, 7ths, 9ths, 11ths, etc., and your stringed instrument can access wonderfully original voicings. Plus, if you play a five-string, six-string, or seven-string violin, you just need to move your hand position down one string and you are in a different key!

There are a bunch of neck diagrams of chord forms based on the note A beginning on page 18. Review them, and try playing them in different keys—all you need to do is move your hand position up and down the neck.

— A Basic Rhythm Part

Try this on for size—a basic rhythm part to a 12-bar blues. Notice the techniques used to outline the chords—the root is usually on the bottom of a double stop with a 5th on top alternating with the 6th, etc. Rock on!

TRACK 13

— String Thang: The Rhythm Part

Try your hands at this rhythm part that can go along to the solo line you played at the end of the last chapter. Notice the techniques used to outline the chords. Rock on!

— Sweep Bowing

This is a technique that I enjoy immensely—it has a very unique sound. What you need to do to replicate it is move the bow quickly over all of the strings in a nice "arch" and incorporate a spiccato-style crispness. The exercise below runs through a number of chords that begin on A.

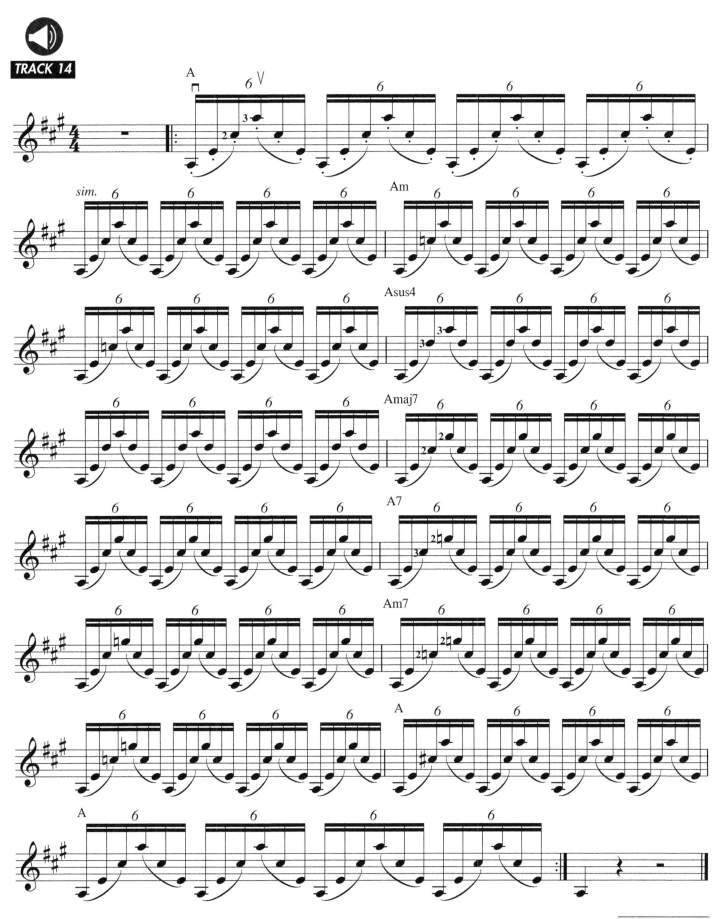

Now it's time for you to fly "solo"! I'm not going to demonstrate this one for you—you're going to jump right into the deep end with the rhythm track! This is the same sweep bowing exercise as before, but with chords based on C. Play this one in 3rd position.

— Down Bow Hop

Here's a fun little tune that features not just sweep bowing, but other bow techniques for playing rhythm as well. I'll play this one for you so you can hear what it sounds like. Don't forget to try it out on your own with just the drums and bass in the right channel!

TRACK 16

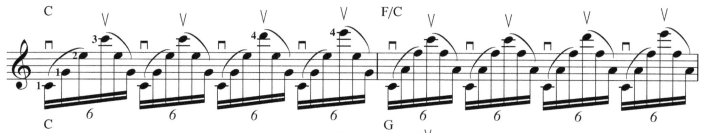

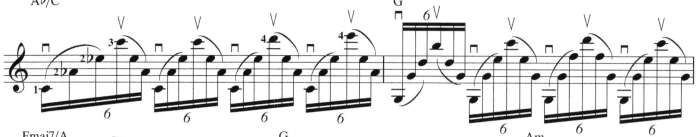

— For Six-String Violins Only

— Driving Strings

Here's a fun rhythm part for six-strings that I call "Driving Strings." When you are just learning how to play a six-string violin, it helps to learn how to read bass clef. This also will help you to access the wonderful cello repertoire, as well as that of other instruments whose music is written in that clef. If you have problems with this piece, try playing it slowly with a metronome, and then work up the tempo.

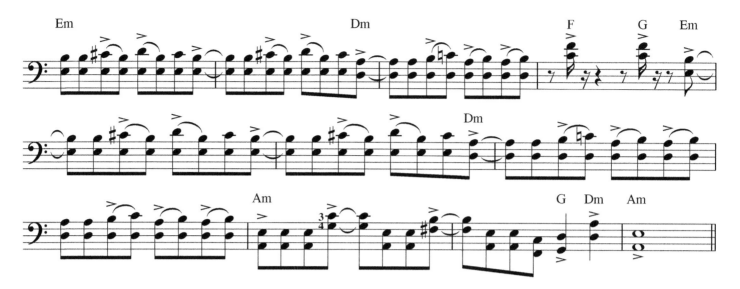

— Viper Rock Riff

Here's another great rhythm part for the six-string violin. Play this one in 3rd position.

TRACK 18

CHAPTER 5

MODERN STRING TECHNIQUES AND PHRASING

Good "alternative" string players need to develop skills that differ from—but build upon—those learned by classical players. These skills include improvising on chord changes, creating variations in vibrato (altering its speed and width), and all sorts of others. By tapping into the strong foundation provided by basic classical training, we can utilize the varieties of bowings and fingerings that give the most immediate access to the various scale patterns and lightning fast bowings most often called for in alternative music.

— Slides

Slides on a violin are *very* different than the equivalent technique on a guitar. For one, we as violinists have the use of a bow!

Since the string tension on a violin is pretty tight, you'll never actually pull or bend a string—in fact, if you do pull one, it will probably snap! Even though it *sounds* like we're bending, we're just sliding.

Sliding requires a firm hand to control the specific distance to each note. The exercises here feature a smooth movement from note to note. While doing these exercises, keep your left arm stable, and use no vibrato. Your left hand should be tension-free—no death grips! The smoothness of the slide comes from a relaxed technique.

Below is a great example of the slide technique. This little exercise on the A minor pentatonic scale might sound a little "Eastern" or "Middle Eastern" to you, but it works great in rock music, too! Use each finger to slide up and down in pitch, and take each little three-note unit in one bow. Transpose this exercise to other keys and scales. By the way, it's a good idea to practice all of these sliding exercises with a metronome.

TRACK 19

This next exercise is the same as the one above, except that you're sliding *down* instead of *up*. Be careful with the two slides that involve the open E string! Slide your finger down to the nut, lift off, and go right back on again for the slide up.

TRACK 20

This exercise on the A minor scale features the violin equivalent of bending: sliding into a note from below. Transpose this example to other keys and scales.

TRACK 21

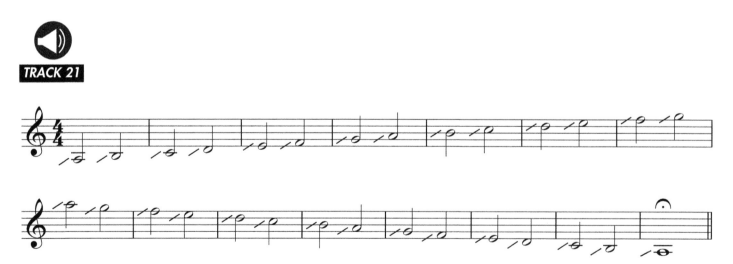

While you're working on slides and bends, be aware of any tension or stiffness in your left hand. Some players actually play with what I call the "death grip." This tight and stressful hold is very detrimental to your ability to be fluid with all of the left-hand techniques described here. So, support your instrument well with your chin—otherwise, the violin will slide around!

— Vibrato

Vibrato is an essential ingredient in many alternative styles. Jazz, rock, and country lines, for instance, all benefit from a controlled vibrato. In rock, you can really appreciate a more relaxed and sensuous vibrato than is often found in classical music. Just listen to the vibrato used by great guitarists such as Jimi Hendrix, Eddie Van Halen, Jeff Beck, Eric Clapton, and Carlos Santana, to name only a few. As far as vibrato is concerned, these players were highly influenced by the feel created by old blues singers of the '40s and '50s.

When I listen to beginning string improvisers, I often hear out-of-control vibrato. It sounds like they're standing on an earthquake! It also just ruins the musical phrase. I can spot a classical player a mile away by their vibrato approach—imagine hearing an opera singer and her vibrato in a blues band! In non-classical music, standard classical vibrato usually makes the music sound nervous.

"Alternative" styles also require a slightly different vibrato technique. Whereas classical music utilizes more of a hand/wrist vibrato with a very regular "pulse," non-classical styles utilize not just the hand but the full arm as well, and make use of vibrato that is often slower and wider, and varies in size and speed. At the slower speeds, the left-hand fingertips don't just sit in a fixed position and "wiggle," they actually slide a bit on the fingerboard.

In "alternative" styles, there is no one perfect speed for vibrato—it's just something you need to develop a feel for. Listen to recordings of great blues and soul singers such as Aretha Franklin, and pay attention to the speed and feel of their vibrato. You may notice some similarities from singer to singer, but you'll also pick up on different techniques, such as playing a long, held note and adding vibrato only at its very end. The recordings of other instrumentalists, such as sax and guitar players, are also valuable resources. If you listen to recordings by the great violinist Jean-Luc Ponty, you'll notice that he uses almost no vibrato at all!

The exercise below is great for obtaining clarity and evenness in your technique at various speeds of vibrato. The metronome setting I use in the example is 120 beats per minute. If you're having trouble matching this, set your metronome slower and work your way up to speed.

TRACK 22

— Ponticello

I really enjoy this sound! Start with your bow in the middle of the area between the end of the fingerboard and the bridge, and then slowly move the bow closer to the bridge to create a harsh, squeaky tone. Adding vibrato can create a sound similar to guitar feedback. Because we violinists have bows, we are able to simulate feedback and harmonics on a guitar *without even having to plug anything in!*

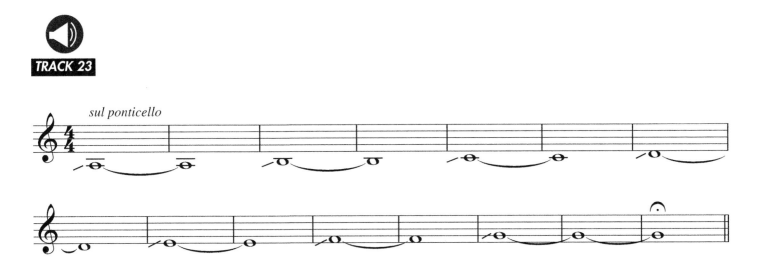

— Phrasing

Rock 'n' roll is about emotion and passion. After you know the basics—chords, rhythm, scales, and techniques such as slides, bends, and vibrato—getting that feeling and expressing it through phrasing is the most important aspect of improvisation. Phrasing comes directly from human speech. When you listen to an engaging speaker, you can be transfixed not just by their content, but also by their delivery. Always think about both content *and* delivery when you listen to your favorite players for inspiration, as well as when you play music yourself.

Phrasing is influenced by many elements, including timing, rhythmic choices, speed (fast and furious to slow and sensuous), tension build-up and release, unpredictable improvisation choices, the use of different pedals and effects pedals, the use of the many sounds that different articulations can produce (sul ponticello, pizzicato, spiccato, etc.), dynamics . . . pretty much *everything!* Having as many techniques under your fingers as possible will provide you with the options necessary to really express yourself, to develop as a musician, and to create your own, personal style.

— Shadow Fight

Here's a solo of mine that shows off a bunch of the techniques discussed above. Once you've listened to it, try playing it yourself over the rhythm track, or come up with your own improvisation using as many techniques as possible! By the way, I recorded this one on a seven-string, but I've included octave down pedal markings so you can play it on a four-string.

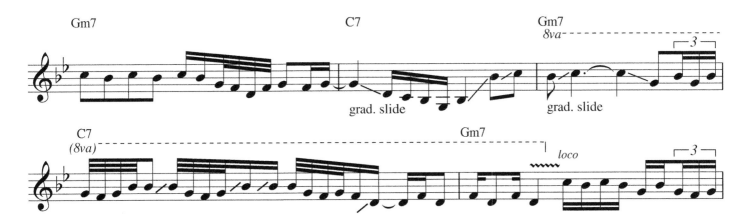

CHAPTER 6

MORE SCALES!

In this chapter we will briefly explore a number of new scales and their application to your improvising. The study of scales can really enrich your playing. Through them, you can create all sorts of different feels, and even emulate the music of other cultures.

— Modes

Modes are derived from liturgical music of the Middle Ages, but today are used mainly (and almost constantly!) in jazz. The three essential components of jazz music are melody, harmony, and rhythm—and the melody often comes from modes.

The modes are, essentially, the major scale but presented "differently." There are seven of them, and they each "start" on a different degree of the major scale. Here they are written out in relation to C major. The first mode, Ionian, begins on C and is the same as the C major scale. The second mode, Dorian, begins on D and contains all of the same notes as C major, but the tonal center is now D instead of C. It's really easy to understand once you see all of them written out, all using the notes from the same C scale. Try playing through them using the octave hand position.

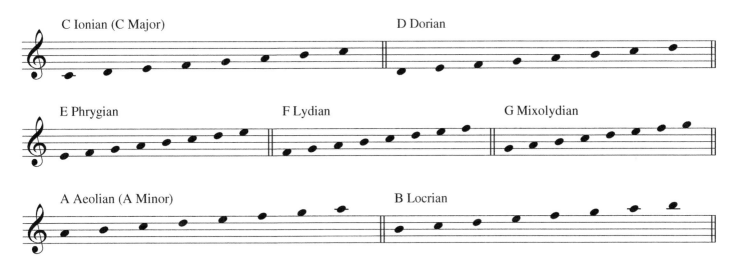

Now, take a look at all of them written out *starting* on C. See how the major-scale pattern of whole steps and half steps "cycles" through the scales? Try playing through these, too, using the octave hand position with your 1st finger on the first note of each scale. You should be able to use the same fingering in most keys.

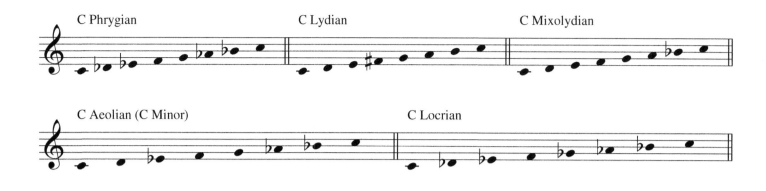

— Modal Exercise

Here's a great little exercise that has you playing through all of the modes based on the G major scale. By the way, you're going to want to play this and the other scale exercises to the beat of a metronome.

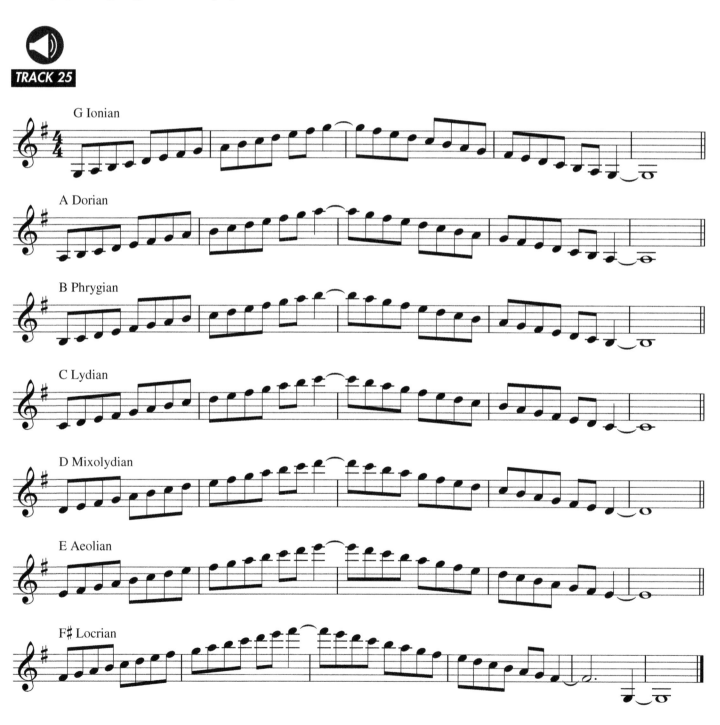

— Modal Etude

Here's a great exercise for working on your modes *and* your triplets. When you've mastered this as written, with the modes based on the notes in the C major scale, transpose it.

TRACK 26

F Lydian

G Mixolydian

— How to Use Modes

Certain modes work well when paired with certain chords with which they share a root. For instance, the Mixolydian mode works great with dominant 7th (V7) chords, because each has a major triad plus a ♭7. So, G Mixolydian works well over G7. Dorian works well with minor 7th chords (e.g., ii7), as each contains a minor triad plus a minor 7th. So, D Dorian works well over D minor.

Do you see a trend? Modes and 7th chords (triads, too!) that are built off the same scale degree, and which hail from the same major key, generally work well together. So, in C major, C Ionian works over Cmaj7 (I7), D Dorian works over Dm7 (ii7), E Phrygian works over Em7 (iii7), F Lydian works over Fmaj7 (IV7), G Mixolydian works over G7 (V7), A Aeolian works over Am7 (iv7), and B Locrian works over Bm7♭5.

Another way to figure out which mode to use over a chord is to choose one that contains the same notes, regardless of key. This opens up greater possibilities for matches. For instance, if you have an Am7 chord, you could play A Aeolian as mentioned above, but you could also play A Dorian, (A–B–C–D–E–F♯–G), A Phrygian, (A–B♭–C–D–E–F–G), or another mode that begins on A and contains the same notes as the chord (A–C–E–G).

You can also just *experiment* and play whatever mode sounds good to you. There are no laws to break here—the Mode Police aren't going to come after you! If you like the sound of something, then by all means go for it.

Now, let's start playing!

— Jazz Hop

Take a look at my mode choices here—I have a very straight-ahead, traditional approach to this C major solo. I use C Ionian over Cmaj7, and G Mixolydian over G11.

Now, try playing this solo yourself using the backing track! When that's well under your fingers, try making up your own improvisations. First, get comfortable with using C Ionian (the C major scale) over the Cmaj7 sections, and G Mixolydian (the same as G major but with F♮ instead of F♯) over the G11 sections. Then, try experimenting with other scales that include the same notes as Cmaj7 (C–E–G–B) and G11 (G–[B]–C–D).

— Johnny Blues

Here's a fun little rhythm track with which you can try out your new modal skills! Pay attention to the chord sequence here—a blues in G major—and pick your modes based on what you think works best. Don't be afraid to turn it on its head!

TRACK 28

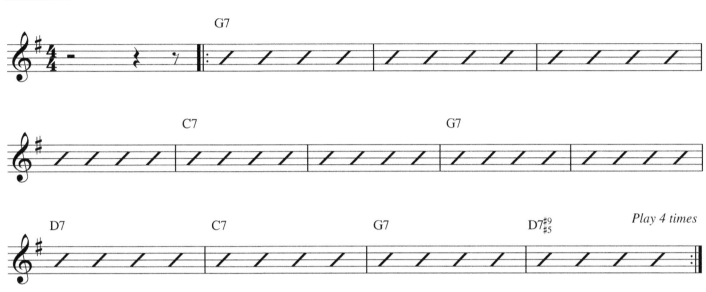

— Exotic Scales

The study of exotic scales can help you to develop an appreciation for the music of different cultures, not to mention broaden your improvisational horizons. There are so many different scales out there, and they're all ripe for experimentation! I've included a sampling here to get you started.

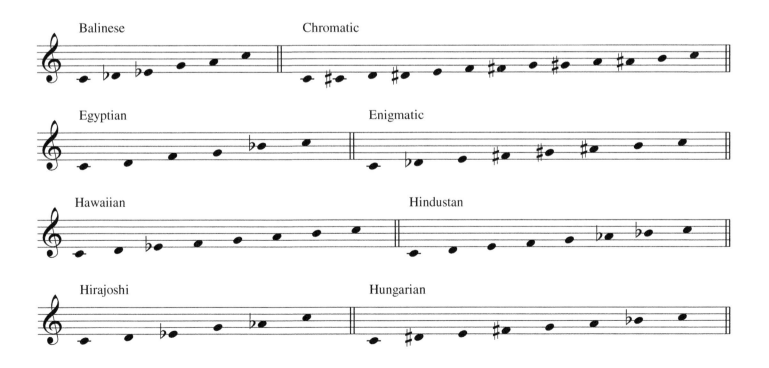

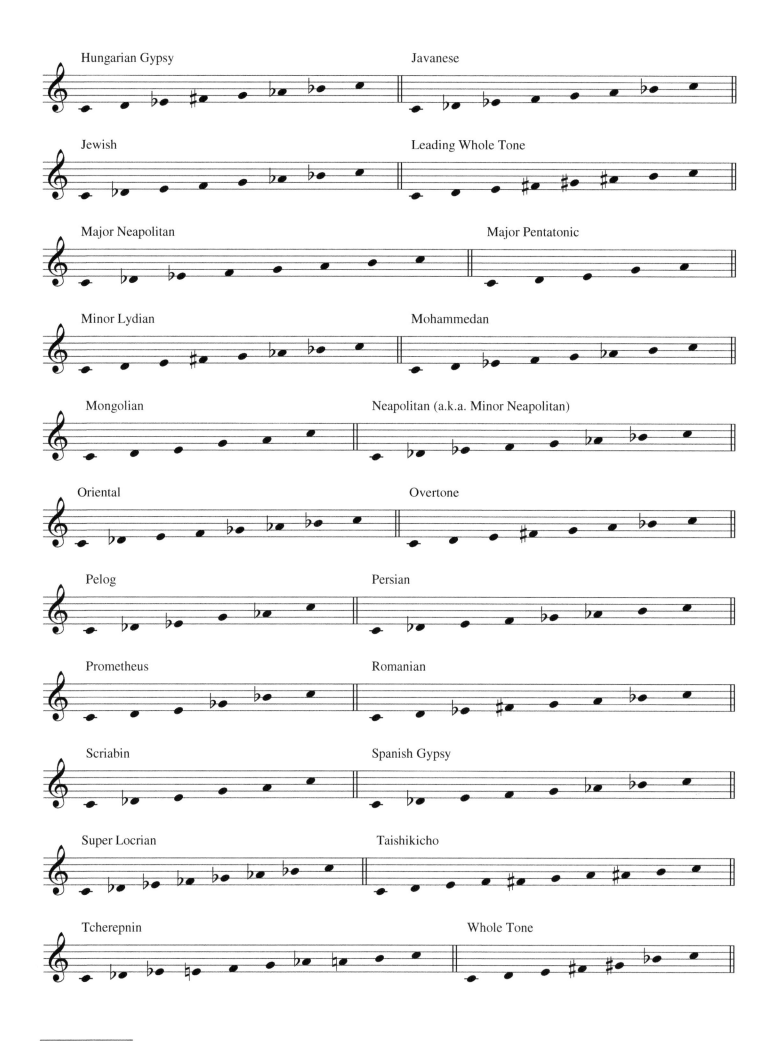

Hungarian Gypsy

Javanese

Jewish

Leading Whole Tone

Major Neapolitan

Major Pentatonic

Minor Lydian

Mohammedan

Mongolian

Neapolitan (a.k.a. Minor Neapolitan)

Oriental

Overtone

Pelog

Persian

Prometheus

Romanian

Scriabin

Spanish Gypsy

Super Locrian

Taishikicho

Tcherepnin

Whole Tone

— Sawdust

Here's a great solo I created on a six-string violin using several exotic scales. You can play it on a four- or five-string instrument by transposing the lower riffs up an octave or two.

"Sawdust" explores the worlds of 5/8, 5/4, and 7/8. Working with time signatures such as these can strengthen your rhythmic prowess by adding to your chops new concepts of rhythmic pulse. All of these odd time signatures may make the music look more complicated than it sounds. Listen to the piece several times to get it into your ear before you try to play it—it may be easier than it looks!

TRACK 29

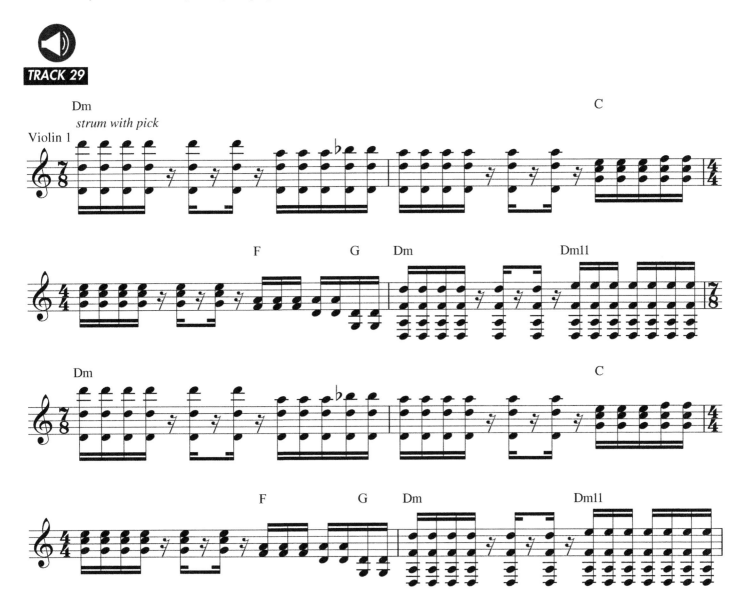

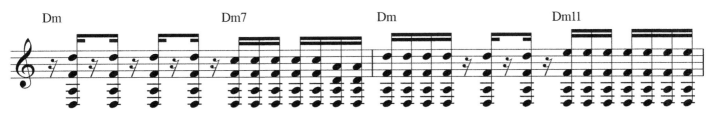

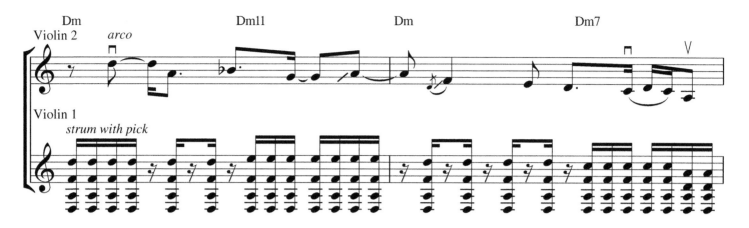

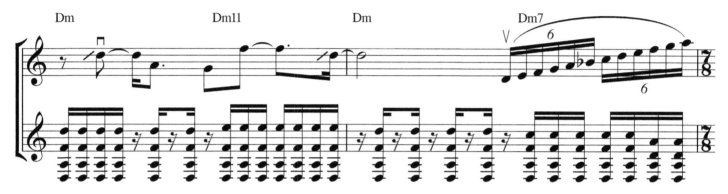

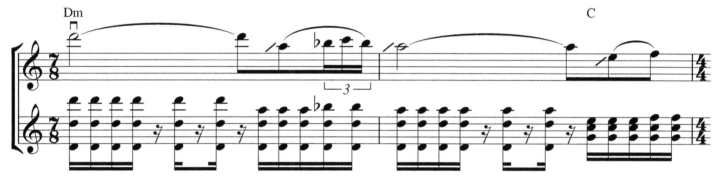

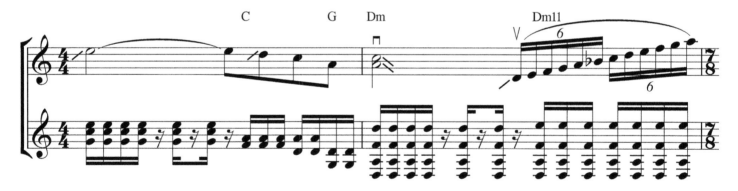

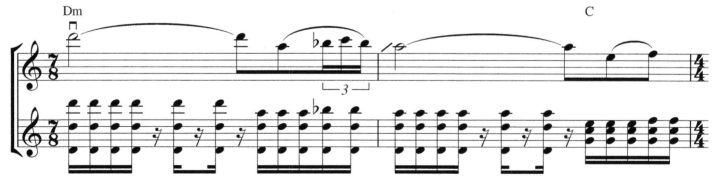

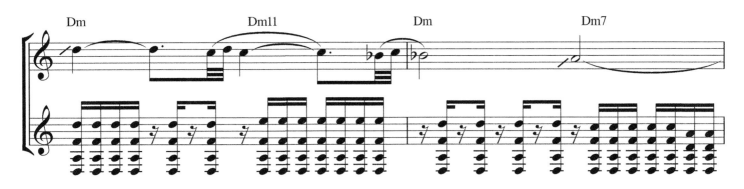

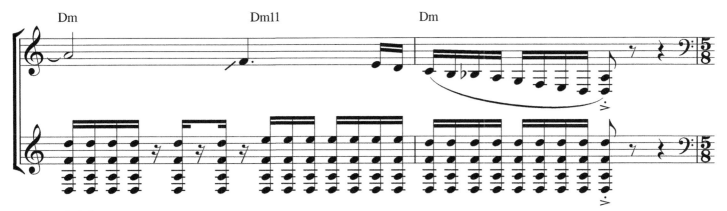

Violins 1 & 2

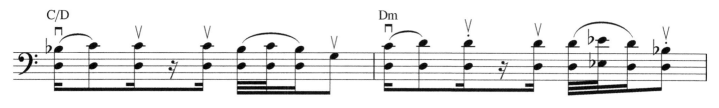

Violin 2

Violin 2

Violin 1

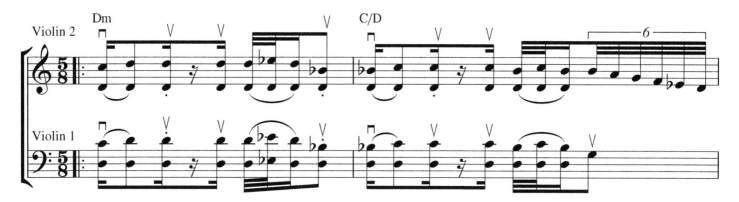

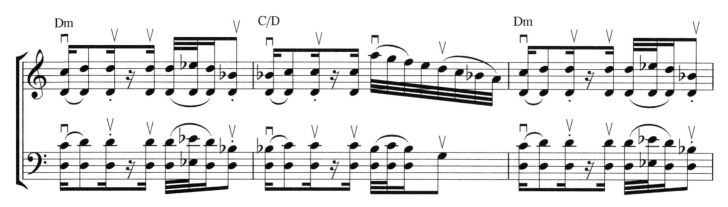

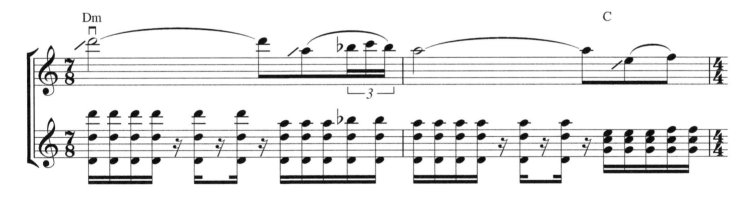

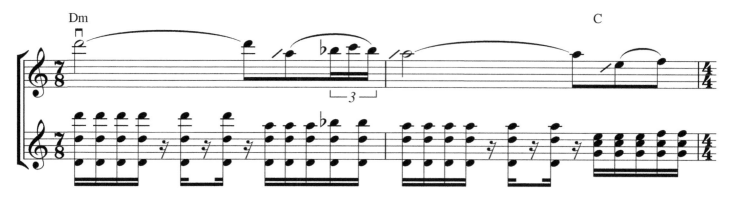

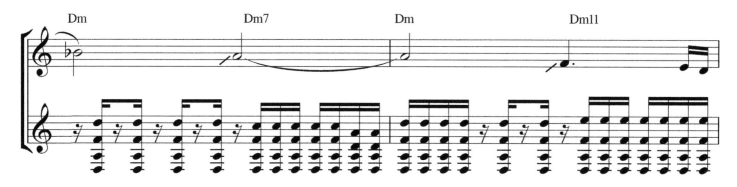

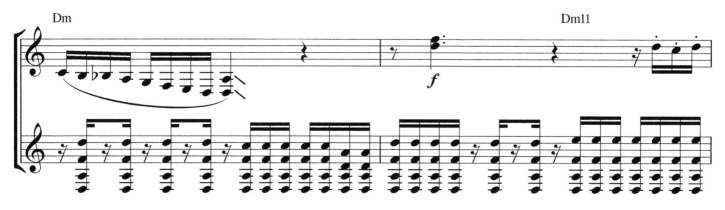

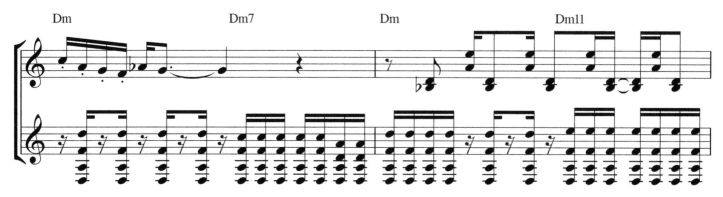

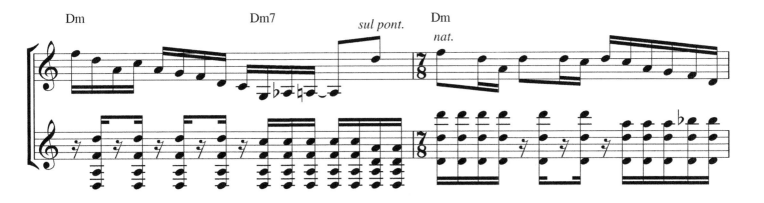

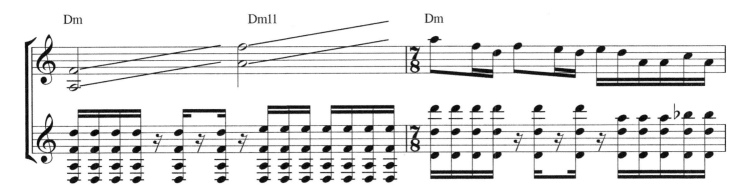

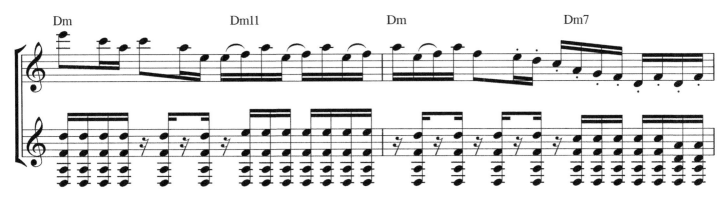

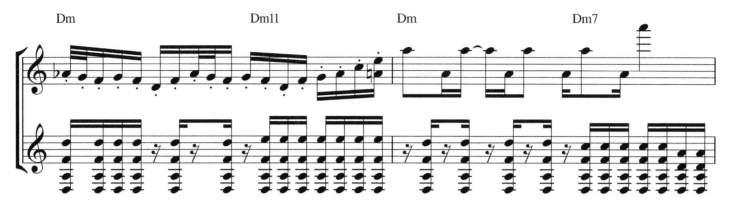

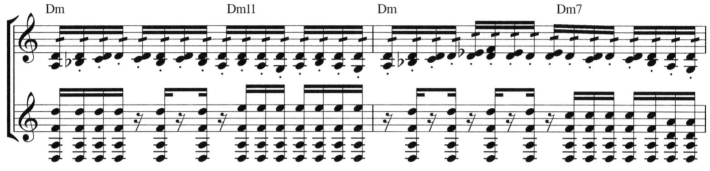

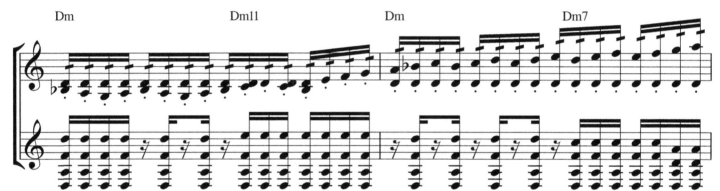

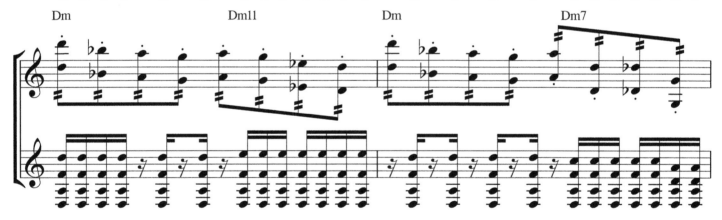

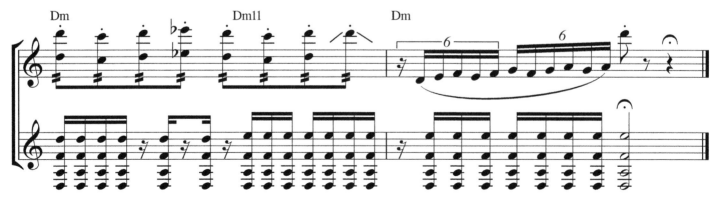

CHAPTER 7

IMPROVISATION 101

When I started to explore the world of improvisation, I found there was severe stiffness in my approach. After studying at Juilliard, I could play Mozart, Beethoven, and Stravinsky with my hands tied behind my back, but when I spent time with my self-taught jazz/rock musician friends and the sheet music was taken away, I couldn't play a note! When we would jam and we were, for instance, playing in A, I was like," Well, I have an A string. . . . now what?!" They would look at me and say, "Wow, you're going to the most prestigious music school in the world, and you can't play!" It was extremely frustrating. The best classical teachers in the world trained me and I could not connect with my inner musician!

Learning how to improvise music is just like learning a new language. And just as in spoken language, in improvised music we must construct and communicate complete and meaningful ideas. To me, music is the great communicator, and upon hearing it each one of us walks away with something completely different—a different "translation," in a way. By thinking of music as a visual stimulus, I may perceive a particular piece of music as "orange" when I hear it performed, whereas the person sitting next to me may perceive it as more "blue." And this is a beautiful thing!

The concept of improvisation can be overwhelming to a beginner. Some people immediately shut down and exclaim "I can't do this!" Yet, if you start with very simple and specific parameters, you can navigate the waters much more easily. You've already taken some baby steps toward becoming an expert improviser—you've learned how to play with the minor pentatonic and blues scales.

I remember at Juilliard, when I was first exploring improvisation, I found that free improvisation—abstract, avant-garde playing, with no rules or set rhythm or tonal center—helped break down the "wall." This was a good start point for me. Then, through trial and error, I discovered some specific stages of training that helped to eliminate the stiffness in my improvisational technique. Here they are.

— Step One: Atmospheric Free Improvisation

This first step helps you to begin to learn the process of musical "free association" and to get your improvisational juices flowing. Put your self-critic aside and just play whatever you feel. Play the audio tracks (the right channels have your accompaniment tracks, whereas the left have my own improvisations), close your eyes, and visualize traveling through space. Create weird and beautiful melodies. Explore your emotions. There is no right or wrong here—no real structure, key, or rhythm.

 Here is an atmospheric "light" track...

TRACK 30

 ...whereas this one is an atmospheric "dark" track.

TRACK 31

— Step Two: Structured Improvisation with Scales

Take any scale— major, minor, minor pentatonic, blues, etc.—and force yourself to improvise using only the notes from that one scale in order (up or down as necessary). Once this feels comfortable, make up a melody line that contains only three notes; you don't need to stick to scale order here. When you have that little line down, try "mixing it up" by varying the order of the three notes—play them in as many combinations as you can to create a nice melody line. Then, take the little three-note combo up the octave.

Here are some ideas on both the three-note and scalar portions of this exercise. Explore on your own with the rhythm track!

— Step Three: Improvisation to a Rhythm Section

Improvise to a rhythm section—some sort of drum beat and chord sequence in the background. You've done a fair amount of this already! But here's another track you can improv over. Have fun!

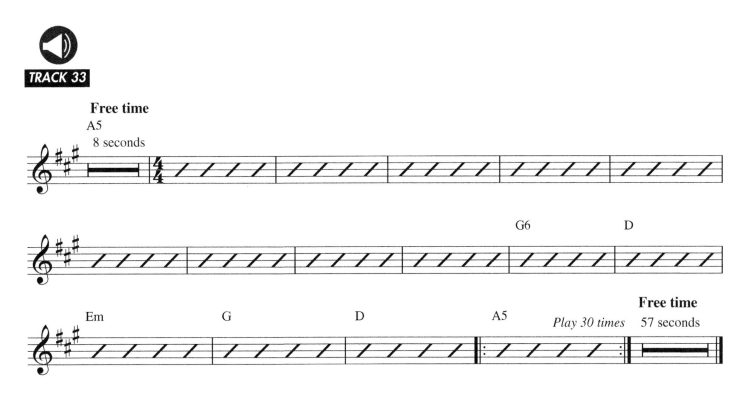

— Step Four: Playing by Ear/Transcription

Take a favorite solo or melody line and learn it by ear. Try playing it on your instrument and writing it down.

— Step Five: Playing with a Band

Playing with a live group can be really challenging, but it's the best way to grow as an improviser! Listen to what the other band members do—their melodic ideas, their rhythmic ideas, their phrasing—and learn from them. This last step is a really big one—so big, in fact, that all of Chapter 9 in this book is devoted to it!

— A Great Improvisational Exercise: Think Small!

Forcing yourself to come up with a clear and well-constructed solo in a small package—just a few measures—is excellent practice. It forces you to say something meaningful and clearly in a short amount of time. When you are playing and jamming with other musicians, this technique is a great listening experience for your bandmates, too.

One way to approach this is to think about how people communicate through speech, and how a speech can be structured the same way as a solo. For instance, in an eight-bar solo, there is a beginning, a middle, and an end—the same as in a speech or story. In a solo, you may start out with long tones and simple phrasing, build to a flurry of fast notes, and then wind back down again.

You can apply this technique not just to solos, but to "trading" with another instrumentalist in a band setting. In other words, you play eight-, four-, or two-bar sections, alternating these "mini solos" with those by another player. Think of this as a conversation. You may try to mimic each other, out-do each other, or build upon what each of you has to say.

— Practice, Practice, Practice (and Listen, Listen, Listen)

Like everything else in the musician's world, daily practice with one or more of the above will help your mind and body to really develop their skills. We are so used to practicing for hours on our scales and etudes, yet we think that improvising should come naturally with no practice. This is a big mistake! We must practice improvising every day to truly experience growth and development.

Whenever possible, record your playing and monitor your progress. You can train your ears to be on the "lookout" for awkward or stilted performance practices, and then you can correct any stiffness in your playing with the help of these recordings. With practice, your critical ear will be your best guide to better playing.

Speaking of recordings, the last few tracks on include some fun material that may serve to inspire you. Check out the following!

"Nine-String Delight"
This is a *previously unreleased track!* That's me on the double-neck (!!) violin, plus some loops.

"Alone"
Here's another unreleased track with me on my seven-string Viper.

"The 2 of Us"
Here's a song on Laura Kaye's solo album. It features a vocal plus a seven-string electric Viper. It's a great example of how a bowed string instrument can be used on a vocal pop song as the only accompaniment.

"Hell-Bent on Violins"
I'm playing the double-neck violin again on this one. That's T.M. Stevens on bass and John Van Eps doing the programming.

CHAPTER 8

BODY LANGUAGE AND MUSICAL SELF-EXPRESSION

The performance expectations of the modern audience have become greater in terms of their need to connect with an artist. The cliché of the stiff and uptight classical musician—both physically and emotionally—is over. We as performers must engage an audience with our musical presence, and grab their hearts and souls with our personal stories. This requires a certain sense of physicality in terms of emotional communication and ease with the instrument. But even if you are never going to play in public, a healthy physical relationship with your instrument is crucial, as being physically fluid (not tense or uptight) can also help to avoid neck, back, and hand fatigue and injury down the line.

— The Importance of Body Language

Body language is an important part of self-expression. Try having a conversation with someone while keeping a straight-faced, stone-cold facial expression, no body movement, no hand gestures—just the movement of your lips. You'll quickly see how difficult it is to convey any human idea or thought—it's almost impossible! Our faces, in particular, communicate much, and reveal a lot about our personalities. There are times when our faces and body language reveal the true meaning of what they want to communicate or not to communicate, regardless of what we are saying.

When you play a musical instrument, your facial and body language play important expressive roles. Nevertheless, some people never move when they play an instrument. This does not mean that their playing is devoid of emotion—some people simply emanate expression from their very being. This, too, can be cultivated with the proper attitude, and is no less effective. Everyone is different.

— Isolating Impediments to Emotional Expression through Music

The following steps can help you to define and work on body language and movement.

Note: Always do these exercises in front of a mirror. This will help you to see what you look like when you play, and to identify possible problems in your physical approach.

Body Language Exercise #1

Relax—this first exercise is fun, and you've probably done it a thousand times in one form or another without knowing it! Have you ever heard of the expression "air guitar"? This is "air violin," so put down your instrument for this one!

Find an exciting recording that you love and set it running. As you listen to it, let your face and body move, contort—whatever you need to do—in order to express the music. One of the first pieces of music I did this with was a guitar solo on the Jimi Hendrix live album *Band of Gypsys.* Of course, I was pretending that Hendrix had a violin. The spirit of the music physically transfixed me. Recordings by the great electric violin players Jerry Goodman and Jean Luc Ponty were favorites of mine to play air violin to as well. The funny thing was that, at the time, I personally hadn't started to improvise, and I wasn't able to specifically learn their solos note for note. I was just *experiencing* the musical essence of each of my heroes.

So, try letting your face express what's coming out of your speakers. This is great fun, and very entertaining! And the more animated you allow yourself to be, the more the music seems to come alive.

Body Language Exercise #2

Once you feel comfortable playing air violin, try essentially the same exercise with the real thing!

First, pick up your violin and bow, and stand straight with your feet planted comfortably apart at about shoulder-width.

Second, turn on a drum machine, metronome, or a recording (anything you can improv to—a backing track or a rhythm section is good) that features a strong rhythmic pulse.

Third, tap a foot, sway your body, and flex your knees (just a little!) to the beat of the music. If you're feeling tense, or having problems getting into it, smile! Smiling is great for relieving tension. It will tell your brain to relax and make you feel good emotionally, all at the same time!

Fourth, play a short, simple riff and cycle it over and over again. While you do this, think of a point you're trying to get across. Then, think of how what you're hearing makes you feel, what sort of emotions it arises in you.

Fifth, let the sound express itself in a certain body movement *while you are playing.* This might consist of something as simple as twisting your torso slightly to one side or blinking an eye. Do what feels right for you, as long as it doesn't physically interfere with your playing.

If these exercises are difficult for you, you may wish to try some sort of "freeing" exercise. Yoga is excellent. The goals are to reduce tension, and to let the body feel free to convey emotion without physical blockage.

— Tension? It Could Be Your Chin Rest.

There are many violin players who have a relaxed and balanced way of playing an acoustic violin with a chin rest and shoulder pad. However, there are many of us for whom this approach will not work—it just creates tension and inhibits our body language.

I've designed a solid-body electric violin with an alternative support system: the Viper. The Viper is sort of a "floating" violin, and its support system allows both hands and arms to be more efficient in their movements. In a traditional, non-Viper setup, the left hand not only must play, shift, and move with ease across the fingerboard, but also must contribute stability to the instrument itself. The Viper eliminates this last responsibility, of stabilizing the instrument, which allows for left-hand movement to be far more efficient and relaxed.

Several of my Viper clients have previously had neck, shoulder, and back problems with other instruments, but have had tremendous success with the Viper. In fact, many string players who approach me about my self-supporting violins are musicians who have had to stop playing because of injuries due to performance-related tension and stress. I am proud that the instrument's design addresses not only the needs of the average violinist who finds the chin rest/shoulder pad combination uncomfortable and compromising, but also those players who were previously unable to enjoy making music on a standard violin due to injury from accidents or tension-filled playing. In fact, a well-known neurologist and orthopedic surgeon uses our instruments in demonstrations and lectures pertaining to solutions for musicians who suffer from neurological problems.

CHAPTER 9

TIPS FOR PLAYING IN A BAND

Whatever the style of music you prefer, eventually you need to seek out players who compliment your musical tastes and personality. Whether you're into jazz, rock, country, Celtic, or something else, any kind of musical performance environment is a great place to apply what you've practiced and learned on your own. This also allows other players to benefit from your knowledge of solo ideas, riffs, and musical phrasing as much as you can benefit from theirs.

When you're jamming with a band, you may not be given much information to go on. Here are some tips that can help you to make beautiful music with your bandmates.

— Know How to Read a Chart

In some cases, a chord chart is the only printed music you're going to get. This can actually be a good thing because it gives you *only* the chords, so you're unrestricted when it comes to improvising and writing your own parts. Be sure you know how to decode chord symbols—what the root is, what the other notes of the chord are, how the notes will move from one chord to another, how chords resolve, etc.

— Know How to Figure Out the Key

In some more casual situations (for instance, you're asked to sit in with a band), you may be handed a chord chart, but the band isn't playing in the key listed, or the chords are indicated by numbers instead of letters (say, "I" instead of "C" and "iii7" instead of "Em7"). If you don't know the key (or somehow "lost" it while playing!), the bass line is a good starting point, as often bassists will play a lot of roots and 5ths of chords. For those situations where you're not given much of *anything* to go on, be sure you can pick out common progressions, whether a chord is major or minor, extensions (7ths, 9ths, etc.), and the like. If your ear training isn't up to snuff, working with a band is *perfect* for developing your ear!!

— Try to Play by Ear and Instinct

Don't rely so much on the music in front of you. Using your ears is the best way to find your way around the music being played, and how you can fit into what's going on. If you are not listening to what's going on around you, you are missing the magic! If you think it sounds bad, it probably *is* bad.

— Don't Be Afraid to Work on Your Solo Ideas

A good band rehearsal will give you (and everyone else in the band) both the time and support needed to develop your voice through improvising. Don't be afraid to try out new ideas. Follow them, see where they go! You may be amazed!

— Listen to Your Role Models for Ideas

Listening to your favorite players and music is important to your development as a musician. Take what you enjoy, and analyze what you like about it, what in the music excites you. Try modeling a riff or solo (or more) of your own on that idea. Inspiration comes in many forms. An idea from a favorite band, guitarist, violinist, etc, can be life changing!

— Record Your Practice Sessions!

I've saved the most important tip for last. It's one I mentioned in passing in a previous chapter, but it bears repeating.

Listening to recordings of your performances and practice sessions is *crucial* to your musical development. It enables you to listen objectively (or at least as objectively as possible) to your playing, and the development of your inner "critic" is the key to success. When I was first learning how to improvise, I was surprised to find out that what I had thought was a cool solo did not come across that way on the recording! Sometimes what "feels" good when you play isn't so great from the perspective of the listener. By recording and listening back to yourself as much as possible, you can close the gap between what "feels" good and what *sounds* good.

Another benefit to recording your sessions is what I like to call the "art of mistakes." This concept is based on how our slips and bursts from the subconscious into our playing can create some of our best moments. For instance, a keyboard player might accidentally change key or hit a wrong note while the drummer goes from a 4/4 time signature to 5/4. During this time, you might keep playing without hearing the slip-up. What you're playing might sound wrong to you at the time, but while listening to it later, a moment of magic may appear! Always let yourself be available and relaxed enough to let moments like this happen—they may lead to some truly beautiful music-making!

CHAPTER 10

FOR THE TEACHERS AND LEADERS OF STRING GROUPS EVERYWHERE: ROCK YOUR ORCHESTRA!

For teachers and students alike, working with electric string instruments in an orchestral setting for the first time is exciting. I personally have developed dozens of "rock" orchestras for schools all over the country, and have received tremendous support from both teachers and students alike.

— An Overview of the Process

The model for this type of configuration is simple. First, we bring together the combination of electric strings and acoustic strings plus, if available, guitar, bass, keyboards, percussion, and drums. We then add a little technology in the form of a P.A. system for the purpose of mixing; most schools have some type of P.A. system already in place.

Lastly, with the inclusion of the audiovisual department (the AV Club!) or the stage crew, we can involve the non-music students in the production aspects with lights, sound, and so on. This can also open the door to including the more technologically-minded kids with the use of computers, as well as software and hardware samplers, looping devices, and effects. The result is an exciting, cutting-edge concert experience for both performers and audience alike.

— Combining Electric and Acoustic Strings

Combining electric and acoustic strings into one ensemble creates interesting colors. But having an ensemble comprised solely of electric strings is not just unnecessary, it's impractical, and actually undesirable, as it limits the palette of sounds possible in the early stages of the game. When dealing with a more advanced ensemble of electric players, an all-electric ensemble can make for some cool sounds and textures. But in the early stages, by balancing groups of electrics and acoustics, a "stepping stone" environment can be set up—the younger, less experienced players should start in the acoustic string sections, and eventually graduate to the electric sections.

In terms of orchestration, it's generally a good idea to have the electric instruments play the top line or "lead," like a lead guitar would in a band. The acoustic instruments should be the support or "pad" for the lead.

— Adding Other Instruments

Now, let's add a rhythm section; the ideal scenario includes rock band elements. By adding drums, you can set up a solid and very audible rhythmic foundation; the strings can anchor onto your drummer as if (s)he were a human metronome. Guitar, bass, and keyboards obviously add the essential style elements of jazz, rock, country, etc.

— Amplification and Monitoring

When mixing electric strings with acoustic strings and a rhythm section, the choice of amplification equipment can be challenging. The fidelity of the strings is first and foremost, so focus on getting a good sound. This is where *Chapter 11—A Buying Guide for Electric Gear* will come in handy. But suffice it to say, always use the best instruments and gear available for your pocketbook.

Be aware that each player must be able to monitor themselves so that they always hear their instrument slightly louder then everyone else; this is necessary for reasons of intonation. Several options are available. For one, you can plug the output from an instrument into a splitter, which separates the signal into two separate outputs. One output can then be plugged into a direct box to feed the main P.A. system, controlled by someone at the mixer, and the second output can be fed into the personal monitor or earpiece of the player. Another option is to plug the main output of the instrument into an inexpensive pedal board that features not only a lot of different sounds, but also two outputs: one to the P.A. and one to an earpiece or monitor.

— Get Your Strings A-Rockin'

The simplicity of rock 'n' roll can be deceptive. We each benefit from the creation of this "rebellious" music in terms of the immediacy of the expression of the personal voice. The beauty of our classical studies, combined with the freedom of expression in "alternative" music, creates, in my opinion, the perfect learning and performance experience for kids and audiences alike.

Accessing the rich and varied repertoire for this type of music is easier than it looks. From the progressive music of Yes and ELP to the rock classics of Led Zeppelin and the Who, arrangements are readily available. Also, the development of original music is growing everyday. Welcome to the future!

General sheet music and piano arrangements can be good fodder for string sections. Have the violins take the melody or vocal part, the violas take the keyboards and other mid-range parts, and the cellos and contrabasses play the bass line.

— A Little Exercise in Rock

Here's a fun little exercise for your string players.

1. Separate your string orchestra into the following sections: Violin 1, Violin 2, Viola, Cello, Bass.

2. Select a key. The key of A minor is a good one when you're first starting out.

3. Have each section go off in groups and assign them to write a part of a new composition. Your first violins can arrange and compose the A section in A minor (eight measures), the second violins can take care of the B section in E minor (also eight measures), and the violas can create the bridge in D major (six measures) and G major (two measures). Each of these sections should be eight measures long. The cellos and basses should set the feel and groove pattern, and establish a bass line for the entire piece.

4. When they're finished composing, the groups should gather and play the full composition under your guidance. The cellos and basses should play throughout. While each section "solos," the other sections should provide support—they should play chord tones in a rhythm based on the groove established by the cellos and basses. Here's a "map" of how it should flow, and note that you can use any time signature you wish.

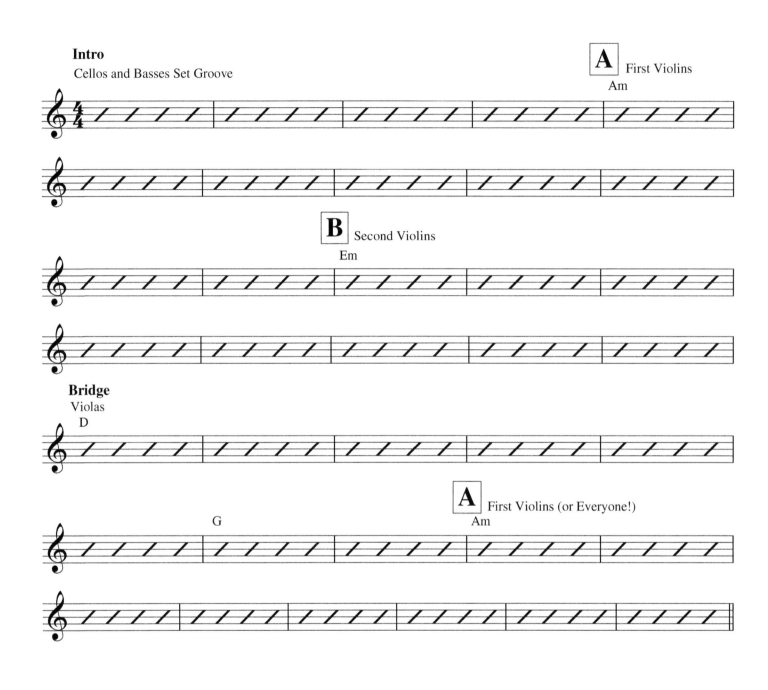

— Another Little Exercise in Rock

Here's a fun one that students can do alone or in groups. Have the students choose a favorite song and transcribe just its chord progression. Then, have them make up a new melody for it!

CHAPTER 11

A BUYING GUIDE FOR ELECTRIC GEAR

Here are some basic tips on gear, as well as a bunch of recommendations on specific equipment, for those of you who are on the verge of making the switch from acoustic to electric!

— Tips for Buying Your First Setup

— Tip #1: When you start to think "electric," don't assume that putting a pickup on an acoustic instrument will turn it into an "electric" instrument!

A loud acoustic violin is *not* an electric violin. When a guitar player wants to play electric guitar, (s)he does not just put a pickup on an acoustic guitar and expect it to sound right. Jimi Hendrix, Eric Clapton, and Eddie Van Halen could never have done the great electric work that they are famous for on an acoustic guitar with a pickup!

The body of an acoustic instrument is made to absorb the bridge vibration so that the acoustic box amplifies the signal from the vibrating bridge. Because of this, the problem with an acoustic violin with a pickup trying to do double-duty as an electric violin is that the electronics attached to the bridge or body are "hearing" only a small percentage of the instrument's vibrations; the output is severely compromised because the vibrations are largely absorbed by the violin's body. The use of amps and pedals is also compromised because the input to them isn't strong enough. A solid-body electric is optimized for output to various pieces of electronic gear; the sound isn't being absorbed by the instrument to such a degree as with an acoustic. *So think electric!*

— Tip #2: Use a good, solid-body electric instrument.

This means that the pickup should sit on a stable wood source that won't absorb so much of your sound. Don't limit yourself to the most inexpensive electric instruments on the market, as you may be sorely disappointed with the sound quality. That screechy scratchy, trebly electric violin sound is a thing of the past, yet some manufactures insist on selling low-cost, cheesy instruments that, when played, sound like a cat being run over by a truck! Nobody wants to hear that—especially when it's loud! There are excellent instruments available in the $1,000–$2,000 range. Your new exploration into electric music should not be looked upon as a novelty experience—have confidence in your creativity!

— Tip #3: Be adventurous with the number of strings.

Why buy a cool electric instrument that just imitates your four-string acoustic experience? An electric should be *different!* It should inspire you to look outside your comfort zone. Imagine having an instrument with five strings and being able to play viola parts! Imagine having six strings and playing cello and even guitar riffs. Or really get adventurous and try a seven-string—violin, viola, cello, and bass, all in one instrument! Wow, think of the possibilities!

— Tip #4: Buy lots of toys!

Get pedals, lots of pedals! Echo, looping, distortion, wah-wah . . . mutilate your sound to the point of no return. Yes, a good electric can simulate a beautiful acoustic instrument, but it's so much more fun and cool to experiment with sounds that only an electric instrument can give you.

— Tip #5: Always be mindful of your tone.

Buy an amp that can process a transducer-type pickup, not a magnetic pickup like a guitar. Crate and SWR Blond amps, for example, are excellent for use with strings. For me, personally, I've found that a good keyboard amp gives me a rich, clean sound, and I can kick in my distortion and effects in a split second, jumping around easily without sacrificing tone. But if you'd really like to explore electric guitar amps, the rule of thumb is to turn *down* the treble. "Screechy" or "fingernails on a blackboard" tones are the clichéd domain of the beginner.

Record yourself so that you can listen to not only your playing, but also your tone. Listen to professional and famous electric violin players as much as possible to develop a good sense of the varieties of tone available to you. And here's another rule of thumb for you: If your "clean" sound is beautiful, then any effects pedal will sound that much better. Plug in, play out! Be silent no more!

— Gear: What to Buy and Why to Buy It

The ideal scenario involves going into your local music store with your electric violin, plugging into everything, and purchasing what sounds best to you. Go prepared! Also, be sure to make a budget, take your time, and take advantage of any hidden discounts: student, ASCAP member, "Here's the price from an internet store. They're offering free shipping and no sales tax. Can you make me a better offer?" etc.

— Amps

I recommend the following amps: anything in SWR's Blonde series, Gallien-Kruger, Crate Acoustic series, Grizzly amps. Basically, any amplifier that's made for acoustic instruments with piezo pickups will work, as they will give you a clean tone and the best fidelity for a rich, acoustic sound. You want a very clean sound to begin with—let the effects pedals take care of the modulation. Also, the pedals will work best if they have a clean sound to work with right from the beginning. In particular, amplifier distortion (i.e., caused by overdriving the pre-amp) can be unpredictable, so distortion is best left to a well-chosen effects pedal or rack-mounted unit.

You can also plug in effects (distortion, echo, etc.) and manipulate the sound however you choose using the amp as a clean playback system. I like to use a keyboard amp with my seven-string Viper, as those amps usually provide a larger speaker for the low end and a nice, bright sound for the upper strings. A big, honkin' Roland is great, but be prepared for considerable lugging.

If you really want to explore more radical territory, experiment by plugging into Marshall amps and Mesa/Boogie amps; they can also be very effective if you're looking for a more distorted, guitar-like tone. On some of my records, I piggyback a Mesa Boogie tube amp with an acoustic-type amplifier so I can have a greater variety of colors at my disposal. The great electric violinist Jean Luc Ponty plugs directly into a P.A. system, and rock violinist Jerry Goodman uses a Mesa/Boogie when he plays with the Dixie Dregs. In most performance situations, I prefer to run a line from the amp directly into a nice P.A. while using the amp as a monitor.

There's another issue that is important when you're looking at amps: the "tube factor." It would take quite a few pages to explain why tube-powered amps are far superior to any transistor/chip/op-amp/modeling/

digital/whatever out there. Audio gear manuals address this to a certain extent by distinguishing among different "classes." We can't really go into the technical subtleties between them here. Suffice it to say, for our purposes, Class A devices are superior to Class B; the former will preserve the richness and sweetness of your sound, while the latter will thin out, weaken, and "sterilize" it.

Because most amps don't deliver great "Viper tone" on their own, you'll want to bring whatever effects you're going to be using to sweeten or shape your sound (e.g., your delay/reverb unit, effects pedals, E.Q., preamp, etc.) to the store with you. Know the sound you want, and bring with you whatever will help you to get that sound—don't count on being able to get the sound you want once you get the amp home.

When you find an amp you'd like to try, dial up a flat EQ and plug directly into the amp. Get used to it, and then tweak the EQ as desired. If the amp has a "bright" switch, find out what it sounds like. If you're getting good response in all registers of your violin, try adding a little delay or reverb. Some amps require you to be ridiculously precise if you want to avoid high-register shrillness or electric violin "quacks" in the middle range, so make sure that the amp is easy to use.

Don't buy anything on your first trip to the store. If possible, shop with a friend who can give you objective feedback. If you can shop with another electric violin player who can play your axe while you listen, that's even better.

As for me, I use my Roland JC-120 Stereo Chorus amp because it gives me a very clean sound without much fussing around with the amp or my technique. It has great frequency response, the stereo chorus is incredible, and it's good for running stereo effects. It's also one of the few amps with which I'd feel okay playing in public without any additional gear.

— Pedals, Distortion, and Effects

Pretty much anything that's available on the market for an electric guitarist is fair game for an electric violinist. These pedals respond to any type of instrument that's plugged in, but a lot of it does come down to individual taste and style. I use and like Morley's Steve Vai Bad Horsie Wah Pedal.

Boss makes an interesting foot pedal called the AC-2 Acoustic Simulator, whose purpose is to turn the sound of a standard electric guitar into something closer to that of a steel-string acoustic. I've tried it with my electric violin, and it gave me some of the upper partials and overall tone that are the essence of the acoustic violin sound. It is still not a picture-perfect replica of the sound of an actual acoustic instrument, but it brings any electric instrument one step closer!

Even now, I'm still exploring pedals, but for distortion, my current favorites are the Ibanez Tube Screamer and the Vox 810 Valve-Tone overdrive pedal. Both are effective in getting the old "British" sound while maintaining a warm tone with sufficient pitch. The Valve-Tone has been discontinued, but if you keep your eyes open you might find one on the used or vintage rack, or on eBay. For other distortion gear, I recommend any product by Zoom; I use an old product of theirs that is no longer made. Line 6's products are also excellent. If you're looking for a great distortion unit and are concerned about tone, look into the Tonebone line by Radial Engineering. These guys pump out amazing products.

We live in a time where distortion is available in so many forms that it can be difficult to choose from among them. Taste is a personal thing, and no one pair of shoes will fit everyone! Still, what was mentioned earlier in reference to amps holds true: use tube-driven or Class A whenever possible. I also recommend shopping comparatively. Sales people can make helpful recommendations, but their favorite flanger may not be yours. Even if you like something, ask to try the other available options so that you're confident you're getting the best pedal for you. It's even worth trying stuff that's out of your price range, just to educate your ear and increase your awareness of what's available.

EPILOGUE

In my opinion, one of the biggest challenges facing string education today is the lack of balance in string programs themselves. The cycle of outmoded classical techniques is being perpetuated from generation to generation without variation, thus preventing our teachers from becoming the leaders and motivators they need to be by thinking "outside the box." But music teachers must also have access to the latest technology relevant to their work so that they can actively pursue techniques that take advantage of the same, akin to the ways in which science and math teachers are able to operate.

We must demonstrate to our schools and communities that we are willing to commit and dedicate ourselves to the future of music education. Many music teachers fault budget cuts as the reason for not being able to take their string programs to a higher level, but with a bit of resourcefulness and dedication, they can overcome the financial constraints and kick-start a new era for their programs. This, in turn, can "break the cycle," and not only curtail those financial cutbacks, but actually encourage greater financial support. For instance, a high school in Cleveland utilized my music program to create an acoustic/electric rock orchestra program that includes improvising and composing, and introduces electric strings into the mix. Not only did the orchestra director notice an immediate improvement in the practice habits of her students, but there were, all of a sudden, large numbers of students from lower grade levels who were clambering to participate! Initially, the funds to create this program came from assorted grants, private donations, and fundraising events, but then the community and the administrators were so inspired by the success of this group that they actually approved an increase in the music budget for their school district. Now, the entire district feels the excitement and the relevance of this new teaching model, which should allow it to grow and flourish for years to come.

We must continue to incorporate the great American melting pot into music education. Music in this country is so varied and thrilling. Our differences and our unique life stories are our strongest attributes. They all define who we are, and we must be free to celebrate our differences. Music education programs provide safe environments where we can bring people of all cultures together to learn about one another, regardless of language and other differences. Think of the changes that can take place because of assertive and creative leadership from music teachers—and not just in music!

GLOSSARIES

— Terms Common to the Electric String World

Band

A range of frequency, often referred to in respect to preamps and equalizers. You may see a band described as "high," "mid," or "low."

Cabinet

A structure that houses amplifiers and signal processors for usage with electric and/or electronic instruments.

Effect

Very generally speaking, a piece of software or electronic device (but not an amplifier) that in some way changes the natural sound of an instrument.

Feedback

A horrid noise often produced when an amplifier is overpowered. You can control feedback to the point of allowing it only when you want it. Feedback can be used in certain bands to accent a poignant moment in a song to good effect.

Impedance

Very, very simply put, it can be described as a value that correlates to the amount of energy needed to properly drive a piece of electrical equipment. Suffice it to say, for our purposes, make sure that the impedance of each electronic component you use is equal. Otherwise, prepare yourself for malfunctions and unwanted side effects.

Pedal

An effect that is housed in a small (usually rectangular) box that normally is operated by a foot pedal or switch.

Pedal Board

A convenient floor-mounted rack on which are mounted effects pedals for ease of usage.

Preamplifier (a.k.a. Preamp)

A device that amplifies an instrument's signal before it goes to the amp. Preamps usually include onboard equalizers.

Preset

A setting on many types of electronic equipment that is stored in memory. Specifically, these are most often found in digital effects processors that allow for multiple tone-shaping options. They can range from factory settings to specialized settings that you or other musicians create.

Signal Processor

Essentially, an effects unit (hardware or software). Often, signal processors are large devices that are best suited for mounting in a cabinet or on a rack. They can include just about any effects and are usually extremely versatile.

Solid-State Amplifier

Basically, any amplifier that isn't a tube amp. Solid-state amps are those run-of-the mill amplifiers that produce their tone through means other than tubes.

Stomp Box

A general term for a pedal with multiple effects. These devices can contain a wide variety of effects, which are generally selectable through an on-board display.

Tube Amplifier

Before the emergence of solid-state amps, tube amps were (and still are!) the first choice of most musicians. They have an outstanding tone that is produced via the use of vacuum tubes rather than solid-state electronics. They can be greatly distorted yet still maintain a level of tonal brilliance that is hard to come by in a solid-state amp. Tube pre-amps can mimic this effect to a certain degree.

— Effects Common to the Electric String World

Acoustic Simulator

A device much like an equalizer, whose main purpose is to emphasize the brilliance of a tone. I recommend one for use with an instrument utilizing a piezo pickup (such as the Viper).

Amp Modeler

A piece of effects hardware or software that seeks to recreate the tone of a certain amp. Certain amplifiers over the years have had a very distinctive sound that is nearly impossible to replicate on another amplifier.

Bass Boost

An effect that boosts the low frequencies of an instrument.

Chorus

An effect that takes the sound of one instrument and makes it sound as if it were several or many actually playing. This effect (my personal favorite) is a lot rolled into one. It is, in one sense, a type of delay effect. I use it to create a kind of "fuzz" and reverberation around the tone.

Compressor

An effect that reduces the dynamic range of a sound. It's often used to get rid of unwanted background noise on a recording.

Crunch

Another name for distortion or overdrive; it is often referred to as such in the on-board distortion functions on an amplifier.

Delay

An effect which, in essence, delays sound from being outputted through an amplifier for a given period of time, which is usually controllable via a knob on the pedal. One can conceivably perform a sort of duet with oneself using delay.

Distortion

An effect that takes the signal of an instrument and wildly changes the amplitude of the sound, which often results in residual "noise" which sounds distorted (hence the name). Distortion is an absolute staple in metal music. There are tons of different types of distortion units on the market, all boasting different sounds and qualities. Popular types include blues, classic, grunge, and metal.

Envelope Generator

An effect that can apply changes to the variables of your sound, such as pitch and loudness, over time. It can be used to create a sort of "automatic" wah-wah effect.

Equalizer

An effect that "equals out" the tonal characteristics of a sound, preferably before the signal reaches your amplifier and other effects. Basically, it can be used to boost or diminish the overall "force" of a frequency range (or ranges) of your sound (e.g., high, mid, and low). It's also known as *EQ*.

Flanger

An effect that can, among other things, pan the signal of your instrument between two (or more) channels on your amplifier/P.A., creating a "see-saw" effect. A flanger can create sweeping, majestic sounds that can seem to fill an entire room by traveling between the channels on your amp. If you want to get fancy, it's a type of comb filter effect, where the signal is delayed and then fed back into itself.

Fuzz

This effect can best be described as "poor-man's distortion." It sounds like a distortion pedal, but it seems to yield greater results when you're playing quieter, lower notes. Honestly, it makes you sound as if you were playing the violin with a fuzzy piece of wool or a steel-wool pad!

Leslie

An effect that is somewhat akin to a vibrato. It simulates the effect of rotating stereo speakers to give you a kind of back-and-forth echo effect. It's useful for doing some nifty background experiments while the rest of the band is chugging along.

Loop

Certain software and devices allow you to record a segment of music and then repeat that piece indefinitely while you solo on top of it. These devices usually come with a drum machine installed in them as well, so you can quite literally be a one-fiddler band.

Octave

An effect that takes your signal and changes its pitch to one octave higher or lower than the original. You can also have the effect output multiple versions of your signal in different octaves simultaneously. It's not always the most enjoyable effect, but it can yield some interesting results.

Overdrive

Overdrive is to distortion as echo is to reverb. Like that analogy? Basically, overdrive is a kind of volume control that completely tears apart your tone. It is possible to control decay using overdrive by letting up on your bow. The purpose of overdrive is basically to squeeze more volume out of your amp and get some cheap distortion along the way.

Phase Shifter

For our purposes, a phase shifter is a kind of automatic flanger. A phase shifter has an on/off toggle that will perform the function for you at a given interval, controllable by an onboard dial. The frequency of repetition can range from nauseatingly slow to incredibly quick.

Reverb

This effect mimics the ambience of a room or hall (or even an imaginary space). When used properly, it can make your tone sound really cool. Lots of amps come with built-in reverb, but a pedal will take you to a new level. It's best used while attempting to mimic an acoustic instrument, and on a low setting.

Suppression

An effect that suppresses background noise, ideally reducing it to silence. Suppression has a tendency to soften the edges of your tone. It will make it sound a bit like it's being run through a dryer's spin cycle.

Sustain

An effect that sustains a tone or tones. For instance, a guitar can sustain a chord for quite some time before it diminishes, but a sustain pedal can take that guitar's chord and hold it for as long as it's needed.

Talk Box

An effect that allows you to "talk" through your instrument. In a nutshell, the way you move your mouth and vocalize into a microphone determines the tone. This effect requires the use of a second amplifier as well as a separate microphone. It's been used famously by Peter Frampton, Joe Walsh, Aerosmith, and Bon Jovi.

Tremolo

This effect rapidly (or slowly, depending on how you set it) repeats the same tone or group of tones over and over again. When overused, tremolo can get really old, really fast. You can, however, make your Viper sound like a machine gun with it!

Tube Screamer

A line of Ibanez pedals that can re-create the distorted sounds of an overdriven tube amp without the use of a preamp. The drawback is that you get only the sound of the amp when its overdriven, and not the pure tone otherwise.

Wah-Wah

A famous effect that adds a vocal-like "wah" sound to each of the notes you play. You can control the depth of the change to create anything from low, throaty moans, to earbleed-inducing high screeches with this thing.

LISTINGS OF RECOMMENDED EQUIPMENT MANUFACTURERS

Bear in mind that a person's choice in gear is, at the end of the day, completely their own. Don't let my opinions (or anyone else's!) on this subject dissuade you from getting what you want. A Leslie effect may sound nice on paper, but in real life it may be a tremolo that you're after. Experiment with different effects over a wide range of playing time. Get to know them intimately. Ultimately, it's *your* decision to slap down the cash for this stuff. You've got to love what you do, so you might as well love your effects, too!

— Effects Gear

Boss

www.bossus.com
These guys are big on distortion and modulation effects. They mean it when they say "boss"—you really feel this stuff.

DigiTech

www.digitech.com
DigiTech specializes in items such as stomp boxes and digital re-creations of classic effects.

DOD

www.dod.com
These guys do just about everything. You can cover most of your pedal needs right here.

Dunlop

www.jimdunlop.com
These guys are responsible for the Cry Baby wah-wah pedal.

Electro-Harmonix

www.ehx.com
I love the sound of their stuff. I have several of their pedals, my favorite being an old Small Stone Phase Shifter that is still around today.

Fulltone

www.fulltone.com
They manufacture a wide array of effects, including the Tube Tape Echo.

Korg

www.korgusa.com
Korg is mostly geared toward digital multi-effects processors, or little boxes that do a whole hell of a lot.

Line 6

www.line6.com
This company has an impressive line of products, and is responsible for the "Pod" series of amp modelers, as well as some great effects hardware.

Morley

www.morleypedals.com
These are the dudes that manufacture the Steve Vai Bad Horsie Wah Pedal that I love so much. It's something of a specialty of theirs.

Tonebone

www.tonebone.com
These are top-of-the-line products, all driven by tubes and manufactured by Radial Engineering. They don't need to get "close" to tube simulation—they *are* tubes!!

Voodoo Lab

www.voodoolab.com
This company specializes in a variety of digital effects. They also have a very interesting Ground Control system, which puts a bunch of effects into one big unit—pretty cool.

VOX

www.voxamps.com
They manufacture amps these days, and their primary effects are wah pedals.

Zoom

www.zoom.co.jp
They make excellent effects gear.

— Amplifiers

AER

www.aer-amps.de
They're very much geared toward the professional, and highly regarded.

Behringer

www.behringer.com
Behringer is a large company that does it all: amplifiers, mixers, DJ equipment, lighting, and lots more.

Budda

www.budda.com
Budda manufactures the amp of choice for Carlos Santana. They also manufacture some great effects pedals.

Dr. Z

www.drzamps.com
Dr. Z's amps are updated tube amps for today's musician. Their tone quality is regarded as superb.

Fender

www.fender.com
Fender does just about everything in the music industry, including amplifiers.

Fishman

www.fishman.com
Fishman manufactures primarily pickups for acoustic instruments, but they also make amplifiers to compliment their electronics.

Gallien-Kruger

www.gallien-krueger.com
Great amps, highly recommended.

Koch

www.koch-amps.com
Great amplifiers and cabinets from the Netherlands.

Marshall

www.marshall.com
Marshall is known as the originator of the "stack" or the "big, friggin' amp." In fact, the classic Marshall stack was originally designed for Pete Townshend! They are arguably the most popular amps in the world.

Mesa/Boogie

www.mesaboogie.com
This is a great amp if you're looking for a guitar-like tone. Jerry Goodman uses one of their amps when he plays with the Dixie Dregs.

Peavey

www.peavey.com
Their amps are characteristically very loud. Peavey also manufactures instruments, monitors, and all kinds of other musical goodies built to smash our ears out of existence.

Victoria Amp Company

www.victoriaamp.com
Their Victorilux is a superb amplifier.